Traces of Madness

Dedicated to those who have helped
us think in new and different ways about
the voice-hearing experience.
Their generosity makes a less bleak
future possible for the rest of us.

TRACES OF MADNESS

Text by Fernando Balius | Illustrations by Mario Pellejer

Translated by Richard Beevor and Mailén Sganga

graphic mundi

Library of Congress Cataloging-in-Publication Data

Names: Balius, Fernando, author. | Pellejer, Mario, illustrator. |
    Beevor, Richard, translator. | Sganga, Mailén, translator.
Title: Traces of madness : a graphic memoir / text by Fernando
    Balius ; illustrations by Mario Pellejer ; translated by Richard
    Beevor and Mailén Sganga.
Other titles: Desmesura. English
Description: University Park, Pennsylvania : Graphic Mundi, [2024]
    | "Originally published in Spanish as Desmesura: Una historia
    cotidiana de locura en la cuidad by Edicions Bellaterra."
Summary: "A portrayal in graphic novel format of the author's battle
    with auditory hallucinations, depicted as a monster, and his
    journey to understand and cope with his illness"—Provided by
    publisher.
Identifiers: LCCN 2023047086 | ISBN 9781637790700
    (paperback)
Subjects: LCSH: Balius, Fernando—Mental health—Comic books,
    strips, etc. | Mental illness—Comic books, strips, etc. | Auditory
    hallucinations—Comic books, strips, etc. | LCGFT: Graphic
    novels. | Autobiographical comics.
Classification: LCC RC464.B284 A313 2024 | DDC
    616.89002/07—dc23/eng/20231026
LC record available at https://lccn.loc.gov/2023047086

Published by The Pennsylvania State University Press,
University Park, PA 16802–1003

10 9 8 7 6 5 4 3 2 1

graphic mundi
drawing our worlds together

Graphic Mundi is an imprint of The Pennsylvania State
University Press.

Originally published in Spanish as Desmesura: Una historia cotidiana
de locura en la cuidad by Edicions Bellaterra

The Pennsylvania State University Press is a member of the
Association of University Presses.

It is the policy of The Pennsylvania State University Press to use
acid-free paper. Publications on uncoated stock satisfy the minimum
requirements of American National Standard for Information
Sciences—Permanence of Paper for Printed Library Material,
ANSI Z39.48–1992.

I have only one occupation left:
to remake myself.

—Antonin Artaud

I'm a grown man of thirty-five as I sit down to write this. Events in the story I'm about to tell you began sometime after I turned nineteen. In hindsight, I realize they may have started well before that. I'm a grown man, but I don't feel like it. Once I reached my late teens, I felt my sense of self begin to crumble. . . .

In any case, I am thirty-five years old, and a blond fuzz has started growing around my ear lobes. . . .

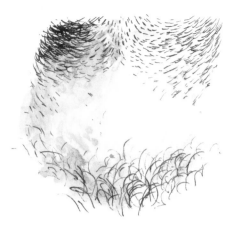

A field of black hair has begun to sprout below my neck . . .

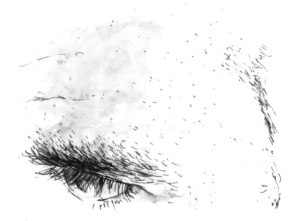

. . . and I've got a receding hairline.

My near-sightedness is getting worse.

I'm thinner than I was a couple of years ago (this is an important detail for my story).

. . . and soon I'll have a crooked wisdom tooth extracted.

I don't think there's any point in trying to justify why I'm writing this. Sometimes you tell a story simply because you want to take a stance. You could also call it "taking sides." I like that expression.

I want to share my story now for a double purpose: to better understand what is happening to me, and to map out my journey forward. These are the clues I started to discover once I realized I was straying from the path. At that point, I learned that you shouldn't stop moving ahead; you shouldn't stop trying to understand the world.

And, as I think of others who are experiencing something similar, I wonder if putting this out there might even help someone else and the people who love them. This story, like all stories, belongs to all of us. I'm sharing it because it tugs at me violently from within, in my guts. I honestly believe that it has to be told. To tell is to tear off a piece of life from so much death.

I'm not going to give you my name. I'll use some clever pseudonym that I haven't come up with yet. If I were to sign this text, I'd expose myself in a way I've not done before. And frankly, I could lose my job. It's true, I hold a reasonably stable job in Madrid, Spain. It's too important to risk that.

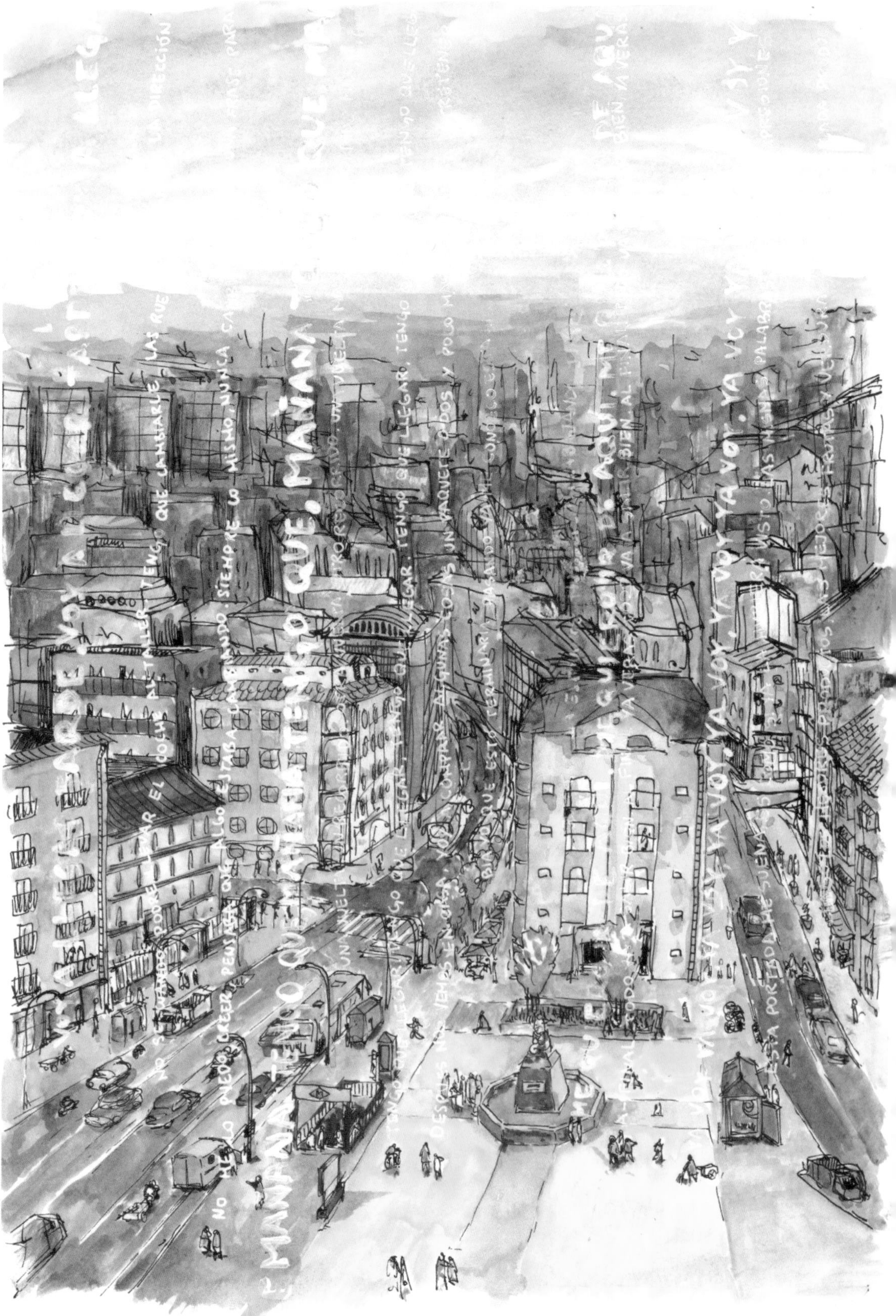
MAÑANA TENGO QUE. MAÑANA TENGO QUE. MAÑANA
NO ME LO PUEDO CREER. PENSABA QUE ALGO ESTABA CAMBIANDO. SIEMPRE LO MISMO, NUNCA
TENGO QUE CAMBIARLE LAS RUE
LA DIRECCIÓN
TENGO QUE LLEGAR. TENGO QUE LLEGAR. TENGO QUE LLEGAR. TENGO QUE LLEGAR. TENGO
DESPUÉS NOS VEMOS EN CASA. VOY A COMPRAR ALGUNAS COSAS, UN PAQUETE O DOS, Y POCO MÁS
ME QUIERO IR DE AQUÍ
YA VOY, YA VOY. YA VOY, YA VOY YA VOY. YA VOY
ESTA PORTADA ME SUENA
LAS MEJORES FRUTAS Y VERDURAS

Let me get to the point: I hear voices. I hear them inside my head. The term "voice-hearer" doesn't sound as bad as other ways we refer to this—psychosis, auditory hallucinations, schizophrenia. . . "Voice-hearer" is merely a description.

I don't know exactly when I first started to hear voices. Up until I was nineteen, I remember only one episode that involved a total disruption between my senses and reality. I was nine years old, and it was summer. It was sweltering at midday mass. I was with my parents.

My paternal grandfather had passed away a couple of months before. I'd seen him dying in the hospital. What was a kid doing in a dying man's room? At the funeral I didn't want to go near the coffin, and I couldn't face going to the burial, either.

Nevertheless, that August morning, I saw my grandfather's embalmed face quite plainly. He was lying in front of the altar dressed in a suit and staring down at the parishioners.

I smelled and heard things that were nowhere to be found in that church that day. I don't know if I yelled. I only remember my heart beating out of my chest and my father dragging me out of the church by the side door. He calmed me down and hugged me. Deep down, it isn't such a bad memory.

You can't say that I had a traumatic childhood. No one ever abused me or physically mistreated me. Hearing voices is often the consequence of a traumatic experience you have as a child. But that was not my case.

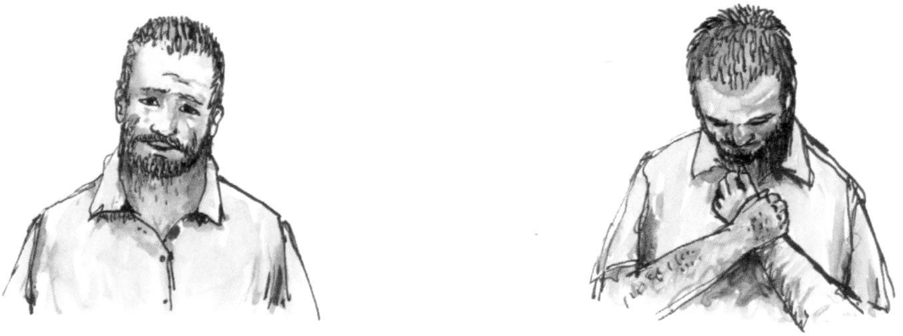

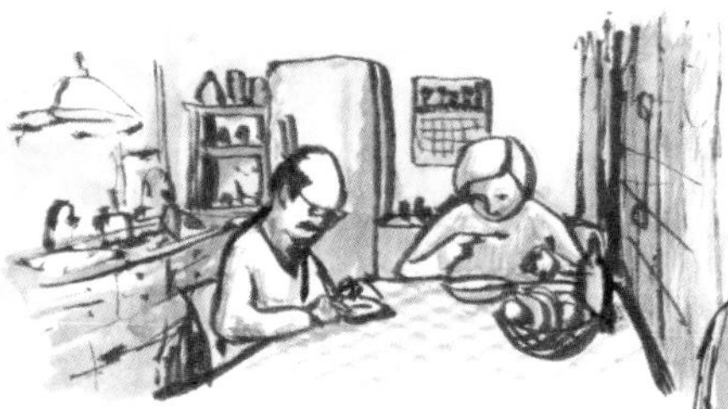

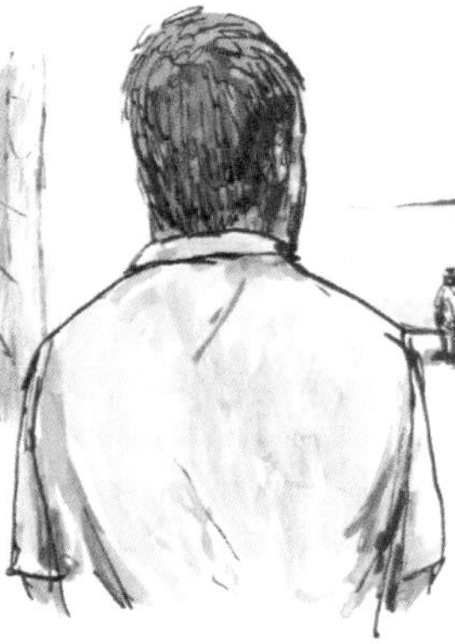

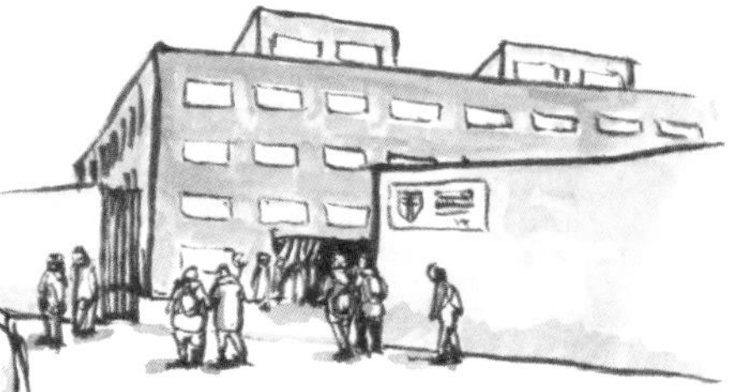

My family doesn't show their emotions very easily, which is to be expected in this part of the Iberian Peninsula that is Castile.

As a child, I never experienced any material wants. I was always well-fed and nicely dressed. I was educated at a Catholic school. . .

. . . and every summer we'd go to the beach.

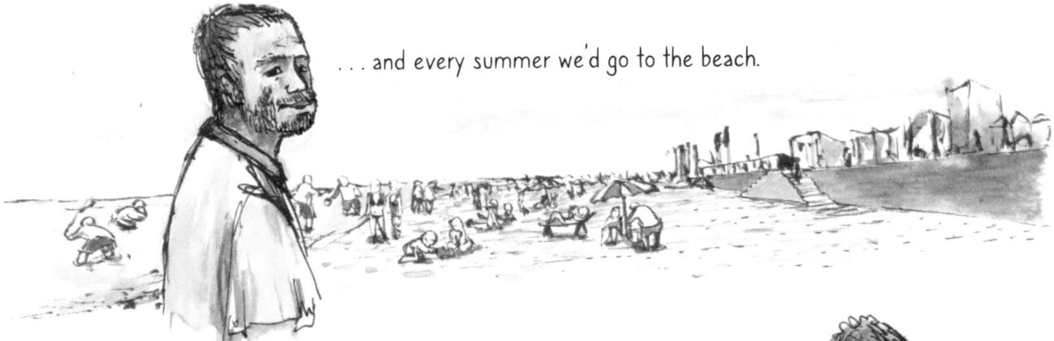

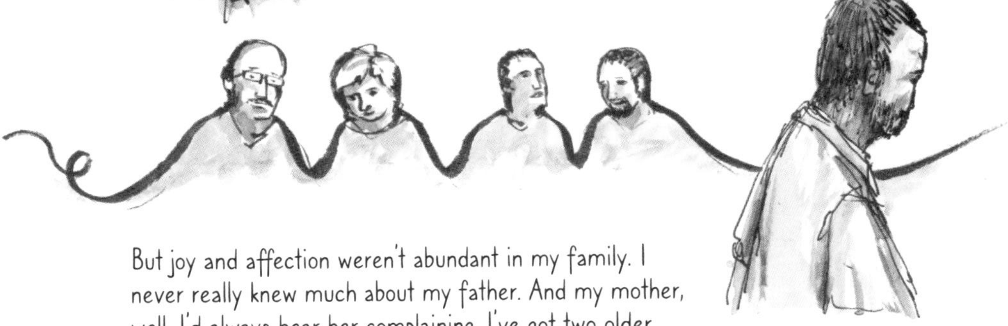

But joy and affection weren't abundant in my family. I never really knew much about my father. And my mother, well, I'd always hear her complaining. I've got two older brothers.

I entered puberty like so many others—looking slightly eccentric and feeling misunderstood and like the world revolved around me: me, me, me. It was even worse *after* puberty. I couldn't find my way, and in the end, I just got lost.

Middle class, suburbs, isolation.

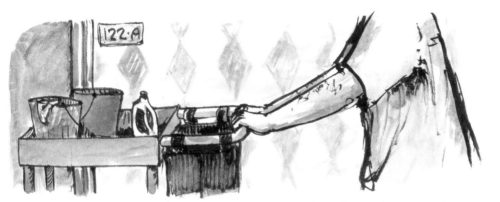

When I turned nineteen, I was going round in circles with no real purpose and ended up cleaning rooms at a Hilton hotel on the outskirts of London.

I went from being a tormented school kid to becoming a bitter member of the working class. All I did was work and think, work and think.

At that age, my head was like a star
delicately balanced on my shoulders.

Little by little,
all the pieces of the star started to break apart.

As the weeks passed, the world around me picked up speed.

Before I turned twenty, I started having serious difficulties telling the difference between what I thought reality was and what reality actually was.

This is an experience almost everyone has at some point or another in their lives. But it becomes a problem when the borders between you and all the rest turn porous, and your world spills out in all directions.

That was a while ago. Sometimes I think that these are someone
else's memories. But I also know that this feeling of fragmentation
is associated with the hallucinations themselves. The thing is,
there's a moment when you can't tell for certain *what* someone
has told you from what you *thought* they might have told you.
Or, to take it a step further, what they *wanted* to tell you.

Are you following? There's only one last twisted step before you start hearing that person inside your head.

The exact mechanism by which our thought gets
shipwrecked is something that, by definition, cannot
be explained. It just happens.

Terrifying? Of course! But not quite like in horror films. It isn't like booming voices are giving you orders, at least not like what you might be imagining. It's something more intimate. Confusion and exhaustion. Peaks of anxiety. Everyday life turned into a roller coaster. Either you don't get out of bed, or your heart bursts out of your chest. A life without a middle ground, with neither rest nor pause.

I remember when my inner stress levels would build up to a critical point. My arms would flail in the air uncontrollably, and my fingers would lash out as if they wanted to stab a ghost. That thing they call an episode—or a psychotic break—is always terrifying.

And then one day, the crisis would reach critical proportions, or the pressure would build up beyond reasonable limits, or something tragic would happen, cutting the brake lines of your thought, or someone would hurt you unintentionally, or you'd be stupid enough to take some drug, or. . . .

Then you'd look up to see a tidal wave silhouetted against the sky, looming overhead for a split second of calm before it comes crashing down on you with the weight of the world. Or, at least, with the weight of *your* world. Confusion. Excess. Madness.

Nevertheless, the real issue isn't the episode. The noises and the voices that are only in your head aren't the problem. Your pounding heart or your rigid muscles aren't the problem. After many years and many battles, I've come to realize that these are only symptoms. And symptoms are clues, traces that can guide you to the origin of the pain.

But when the traces of madness start defining your surroundings, other people seem not to wonder why. That's the fucking problem: they respond to you with a volatile mix of fear, ignorance, and calculated indifference.

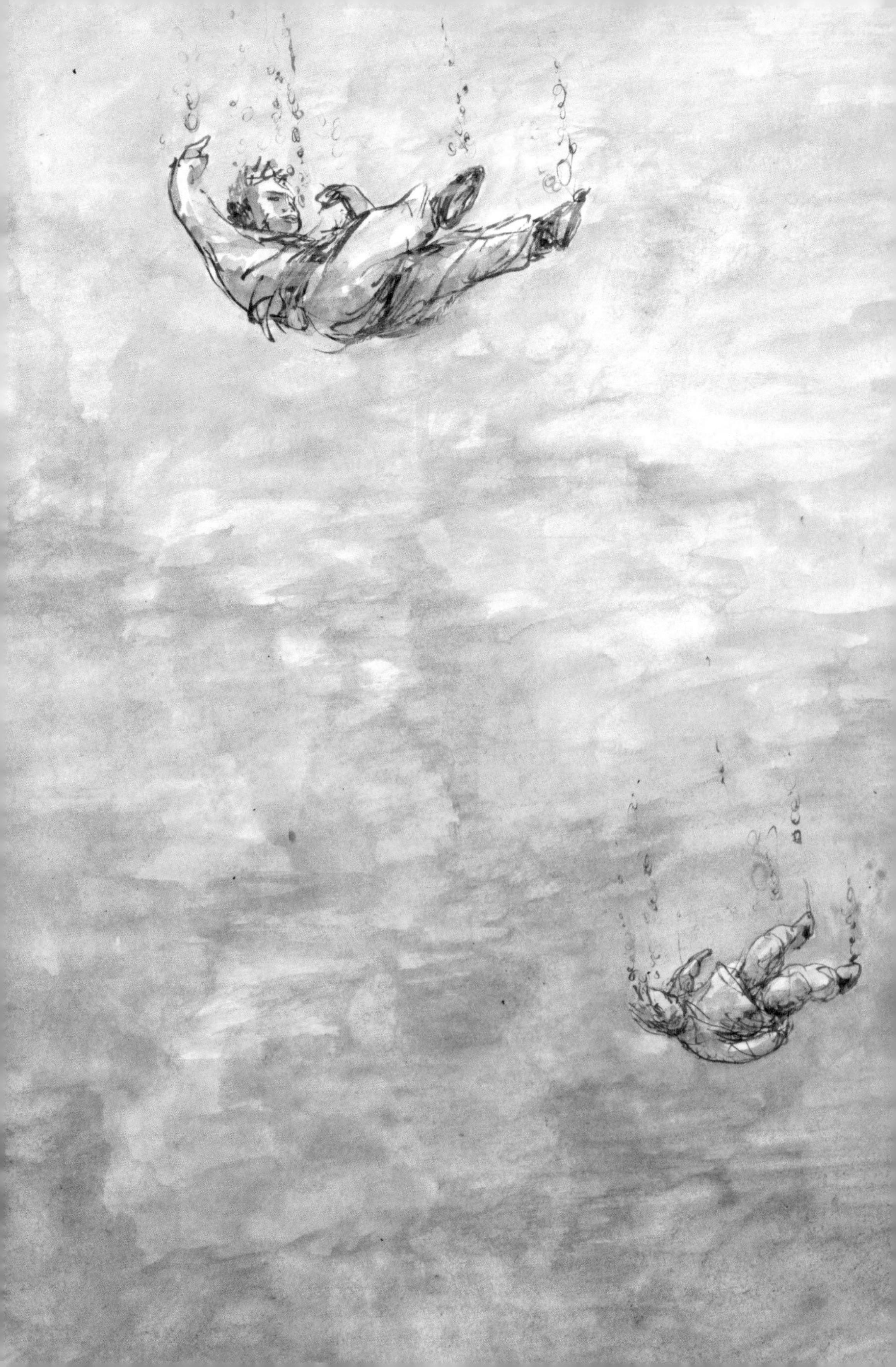

Things got much worse in a matter of months. My anxiety was growing. I was convinced I knew what others thought of me at every moment. A classic symptom of mental suffering: thinking that others spend their time judging you.

It's a selfish spiral that plunges you into an almost hypnotic state and traps you there.

The absurd conviction that had come over me was particularly strong when it came to my girlfriend. When we would go out, I really believed I knew exactly what she was thinking.

ARE YOU SURE YOU WANT TO GO OUT WITH ME?

OF COURSE.... WHAT'S WITH ALL THESE QUESTIONS? I'M HERE, AREN'T I?

... I WISH I WASN'T GOING OUT WITH HIM. SOMETHING'S WRONG WITH HIM.... I HAVE TO FIGURE OUT HOW TO LEAVE HIM. I CAN'T STAND HIM. GOD, I CAN'T STAND HIM....

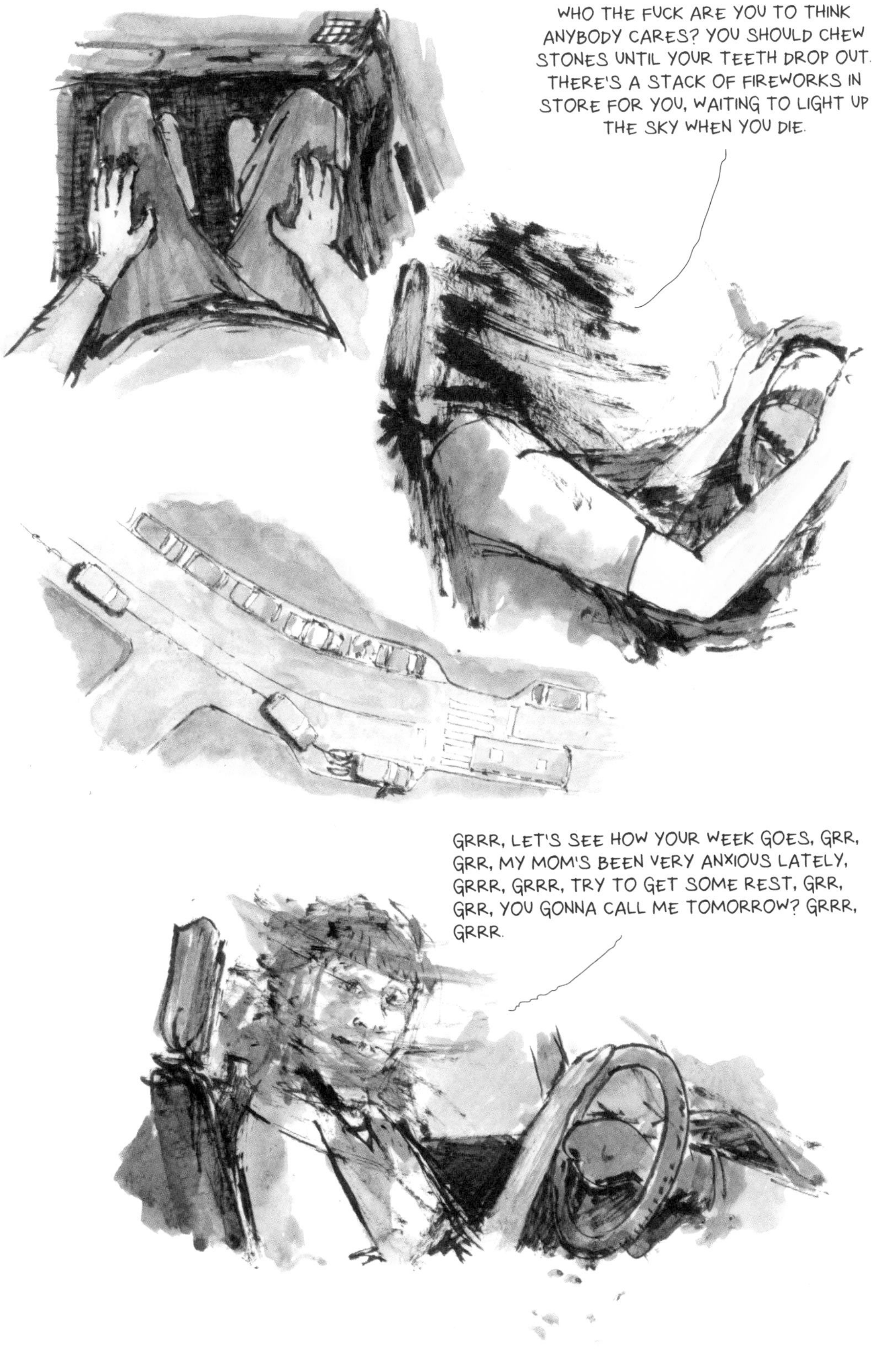
WHO THE FUCK ARE YOU TO THINK ANYBODY CARES? YOU SHOULD CHEW STONES UNTIL YOUR TEETH DROP OUT. THERE'S A STACK OF FIREWORKS IN STORE FOR YOU, WAITING TO LIGHT UP THE SKY WHEN YOU DIE.
GRRR, LET'S SEE HOW YOUR WEEK GOES, GRR, GRR, MY MOM'S BEEN VERY ANXIOUS LATELY, GRRR, GRRR, TRY TO GET SOME REST, GRR, GRR, YOU GONNA CALL ME TOMORROW? GRRR, GRRR.

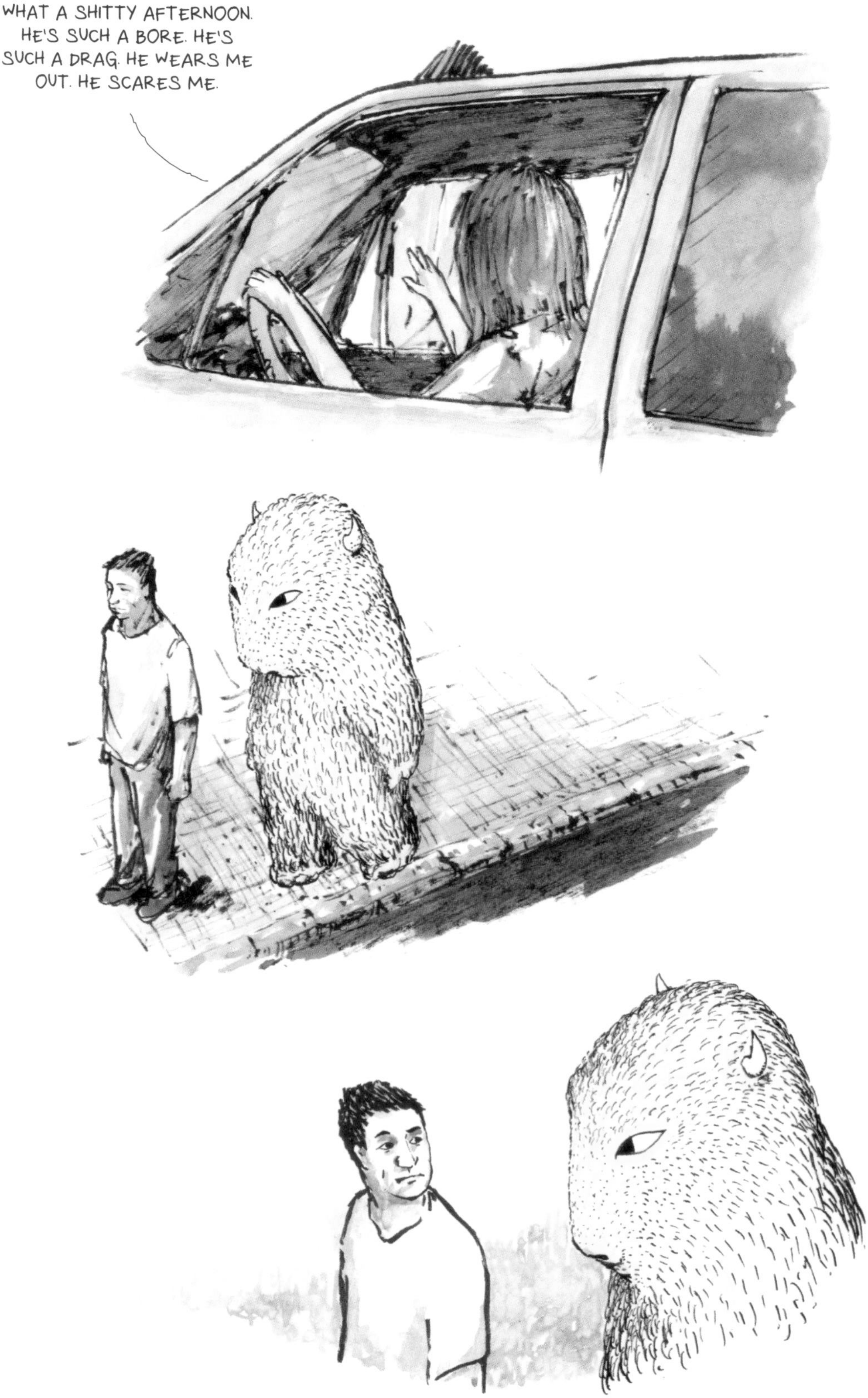
WHAT A SHITTY AFTERNOON. HE'S SUCH A BORE. HE'S SUCH A DRAG. HE WEARS ME OUT. HE SCARES ME.

Something similar happened with the rest of the people in my life, whether they were around or not. I was living in a perpetual state between rejection and reproach. And I'm aware of the damage I caused because of this—at least the damage I could *see,* and the damage that others helped me see.

One day, I noticed some spots on my skin that, over time, seemed to move around.

My GP thought it might be . . .

. . . FOOD POISONING.

When that wasn't right, he proposed . . .

. . . THE MEASLES.

And finally, after quite a few days of this, he asked me:

HOW HAVE YOU BEEN FEELING LATELY?

I don't remember what my answer was, but I ended up seeing a psychiatrist who diagnosed me with an obsessive-compulsive disorder and gave me a drug called Anafranil®. The skin spots disappeared as suddenly as they had appeared.

Those salmon-colored pills didn't agree with me.

I stopped taking them after a few weeks.

I went back to the outpatient clinic. My psychiatrist was on vacation, so the doctor who saw me simply consulted the other doctor's notes and suggested increasing the dosage. But intuition told me that taking more of something that wasn't doing me any good wasn't a great idea.

Anxiety seized me in my guts, making any unease I had felt before seem trivial.

I couldn't stop vomiting. I was hospitalized. First, I was seen by gastroenterologists, then by doctors on the psychiatry ward. I can recall only a few of the images that were seared in my mind at the time— how bewildered my friends were, the aloofness of a young female doctor, an elderly guy begging at the top of his lungs to be killed, a junkie whispering to me to untie her straps, the murmuring of the nurses, the chipped paint on the wall. . . .

I was afraid. The drops they put on my tongue made everything even more of a blur. I clearly remember thinking how vital it was that my parents *not* find out about this. And they didn't. Nor did my brothers. Actually, I needn't have worried about this, because eventually I realized that my mental health issues were a taboo subject for my family. Why waste my energy trying to hide them? They were a nonissue then and still are to this day.

This kind of thing happens a lot in families, and getting upset about it is frankly pointless. It's simply due to a combination of social stigma and a lack of emotional intelligence.

You can confront those two things, and you can try to fight them. But, in the end, change is something that only people can bring about themselves. If you think about it, you realize that the emptiness that settles in around the sufferer is nothing but fear.

Everyone (or at least everyone I know) has at some point experienced something very close to madness. When that happens, it's normal to want to put on armor and blindfold yourself.

My initial experience with the mental health system—diagnosis, then treatment, then (brief) hospitalization—led to regular pilgrimages to my local mental health clinic. And so began the constant changes in medication.

The diagnosis changed. A guy in a doctor's coat and with a dazed expression on his face looked at me with his tired eyes and started to talk about psychosis. Then he began to tiptoe around that other evil word that no mother ever wants to hear: "schizophrenia." He presented it as though it were a threat, something off on the horizon—a potentiality—and, at the same time, also a current reality.

I can't even remember how I took the blow that day. Perhaps I
didn't even interpret it as something so awful. After all, I didn't
know any "psychotics" or "schizophrenics" (I later realized
there are no such things—there are only people), and from
an early age I never really believed what we saw in
the movies and newspapers. My real experience was
confined to just one very concrete phenomenon:
hearing voices. And when you open up about this
to others, whoever they may be, either under
the quiet pressure of the psychiatrist on
duty or simply because you're driven by
a naïve honesty, something breaks in
the invisible space surrounding you.
So you learn to keep quiet. And,
of course, when you shut up
about it, you're no longer
yourself. When you're left
without a place where
you can be who you
are, it's difficult for
things to get
better.

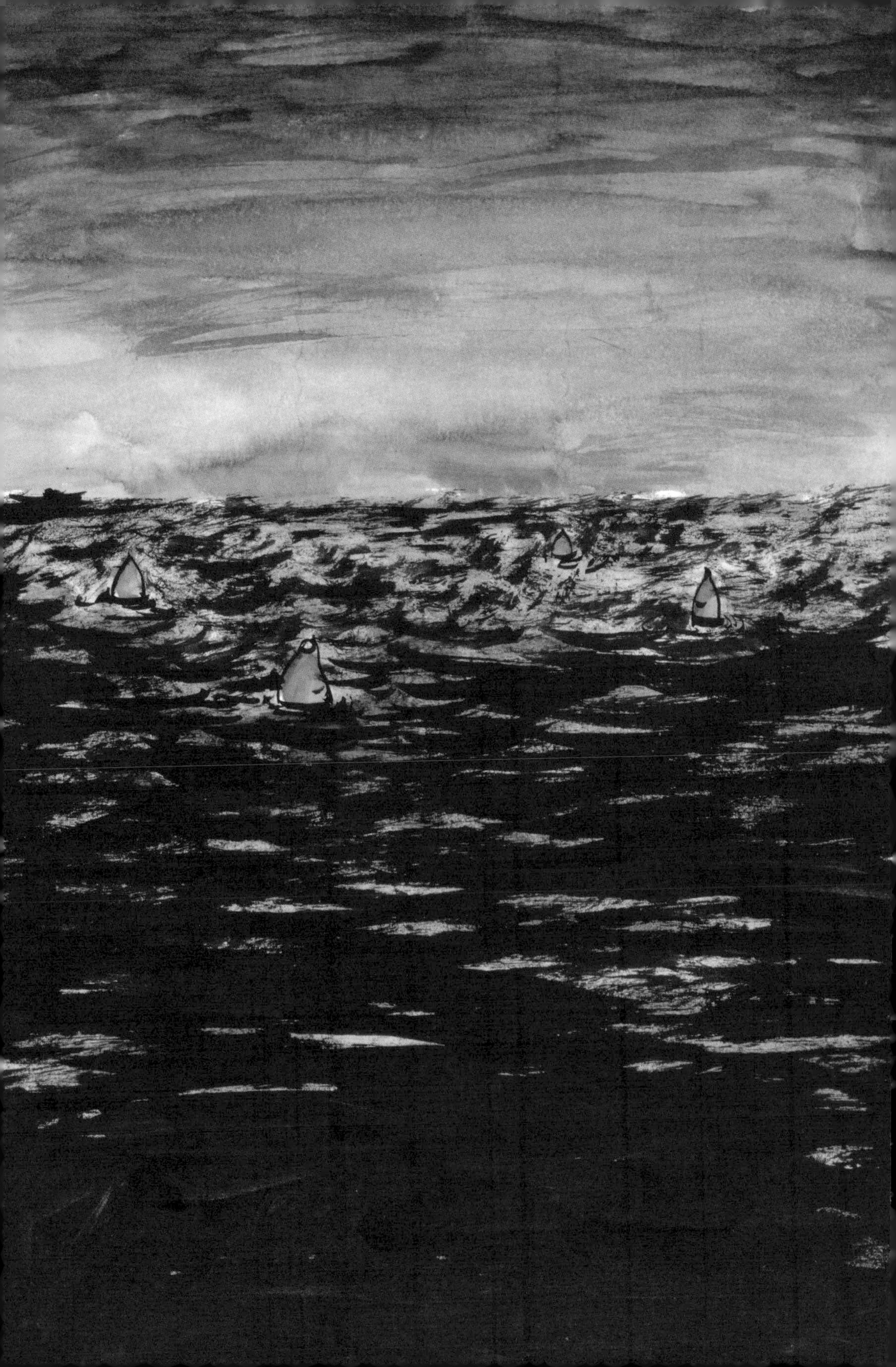

When we talk about mental health or psychological suffering, we naturally think about what's going on inside our heads. But the rest of the body is also involved in that suffering. And that's not something we often talk about.

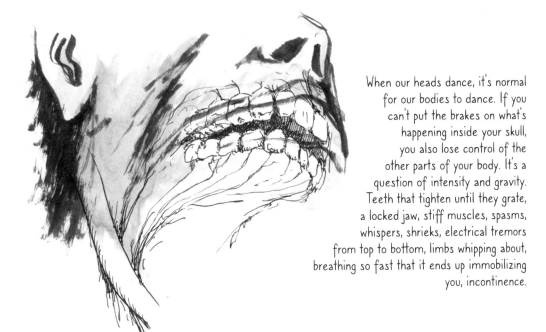

When our heads dance, it's normal for our bodies to dance. If you can't put the brakes on what's happening inside your skull, you also lose control of the other parts of your body. It's a question of intensity and gravity. Teeth that tighten until they grate, a locked jaw, stiff muscles, spasms, whispers, shrieks, electrical tremors from top to bottom, limbs whipping about, breathing so fast that it ends up immobilizing you, incontinence.

Incontinence: pissing yourself or, to be honest, shitting yourself. I was in my twenties when I fully understood the meaning of "being scared shitless." Your head and body are galloping at full speed in all directions, and you're trying desperately not to lose yourself. But halfway through the delirium, a part of you starts contemplating the very real possibility that you won't be able to come back from this once you're fully lost. You'll be lost for good.

This is how you stop being in control of your sphincter, and you shit your pants.

Anyway, I think that this unavoidably heavy burden must be seen for exactly what it is: terrible. Just like many other things in the lives of many other people.

What's really fucked up isn't losing your head; it's the fact that there's nobody around when you try to get it back.

I'm a lucky man. Many times, while coming back, I was able to see and feel my people close by.

The word "love" is used unconsciously.
Love means weathering the storm *together*.

It doesn't matter whether you're doing it with your partner, your
friend, your lover, or your neighbor. Love means standing firm. So
that when the other comes back, he finds himself in bed with clean
clothes, a clean bum, and warm eyes watching over him. There's
nothing to be grateful for nor to feel guilty about. Nothing to
reproach. No scores to settle. We are where we want to be.

These are the moments I cherish—not the others. I don't
remember much about the others. Disconnected scraps, feelings,
sometimes even smells.

I keep them in mind on purpose. These are my treasures and my
health. If you want to get technical about it, it's pure strategy. You
must have a refuge the next time the thunderous black clouds head
your way . . .

. . . and love and humor are my refuge. It wasn't
easy to find them. I've made them my own, and I
guard them carefully.

For someone who hears voices, incorporating humor into your daily life is *vital.* I dare say it's the same for anyone who is suffering from some sort of mental health problem. If you don't laugh a little about yourself, there is no hope.

The places we're typically dragged to by our cultural conceptions of madness are . . . heartbreaking.

Isolation and torment. An interminably adolescent and selfish form of damnation.

Please understand how hard it is to fight back from such a place. It's much easier to defend yourself in open spaces. I know from first-hand experience.

When I talk about humor and madness, I'm in no way suggesting that we ridicule those who are having a bad time. I once saw a young neurologist chatting over beers with some other doctors and mimicking a psychotic break she had witnessed in the hospital emergency department. Deep noisy chuckles. It was only common sense that stopped me from throwing a bottle at them.

That's not good humor. At work, it's not good humor when I have some kind of involuntary gesture— I wink an eye and shake my hand at shoulder height—and a colleague sitting next to me asks, giggling, if I remembered to take my meds today. It's a running joke. One time I tried answering: "No, I haven't been on antipsychotics for years." To no effect. Nobody heard, and the conversation went on.

I'm talking about a different kind of humor: health-humor. Humor we can use as an instrument in the pursuit of good health. The kind of comment that is a spark that lights a dark room, or a tall glass of cool, clear water that somebody offers you when you're thirsty.

Memorable moments.

I was a student sharing a flat with four other guys who were just as broke as me. I was happy living with them.

After dinner, without warning, I had a break (or an episode, an attack, a fit, a spell). I was eating a yogurt in the kitchen.

That was all I could remember once I was able to get out of bed the next morning: I had sat down to have breakfast with the others, and then I was completely out of it.

There was an awkward silence. I waved hello and mechanically poured myself a cup of coffee. One of my friends, looking very serious, started to speak in a grave voice.

WE NEED TO TALK....

THIS HAS TO STOP.

I MEAN, IT'S SUPER COOL THAT YOU CAN BE YOURSELF AND ALL THAT.

IT'S OKAY IF YOU LIKE ART...

... BUT IF YOU'RE GOING TO HAVE A FUCKING HAPPENING, PERFORMANCE ART, OR ONE OF THOSE HIPPIE THINGS...

... THEN CLEAN UP AFTER YOURSELF, FOR FUCK'S SAKE!

We laughed so hard that coffee went flying everywhere, probably just like the yogurt did the night before. That was it, we moved on. I was among family.

There were also moments of more intimate humor. The kind
of humor shared by two people that results in an evening of
continuous laughter that you both hope will never come to an end.

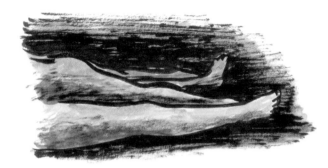

Humor sabotages the sick ways
we engage with the world.

Humor lifts tension and gets you out of your head.
It dilutes your ego. It makes you less stupid and helps
you feel grounded.

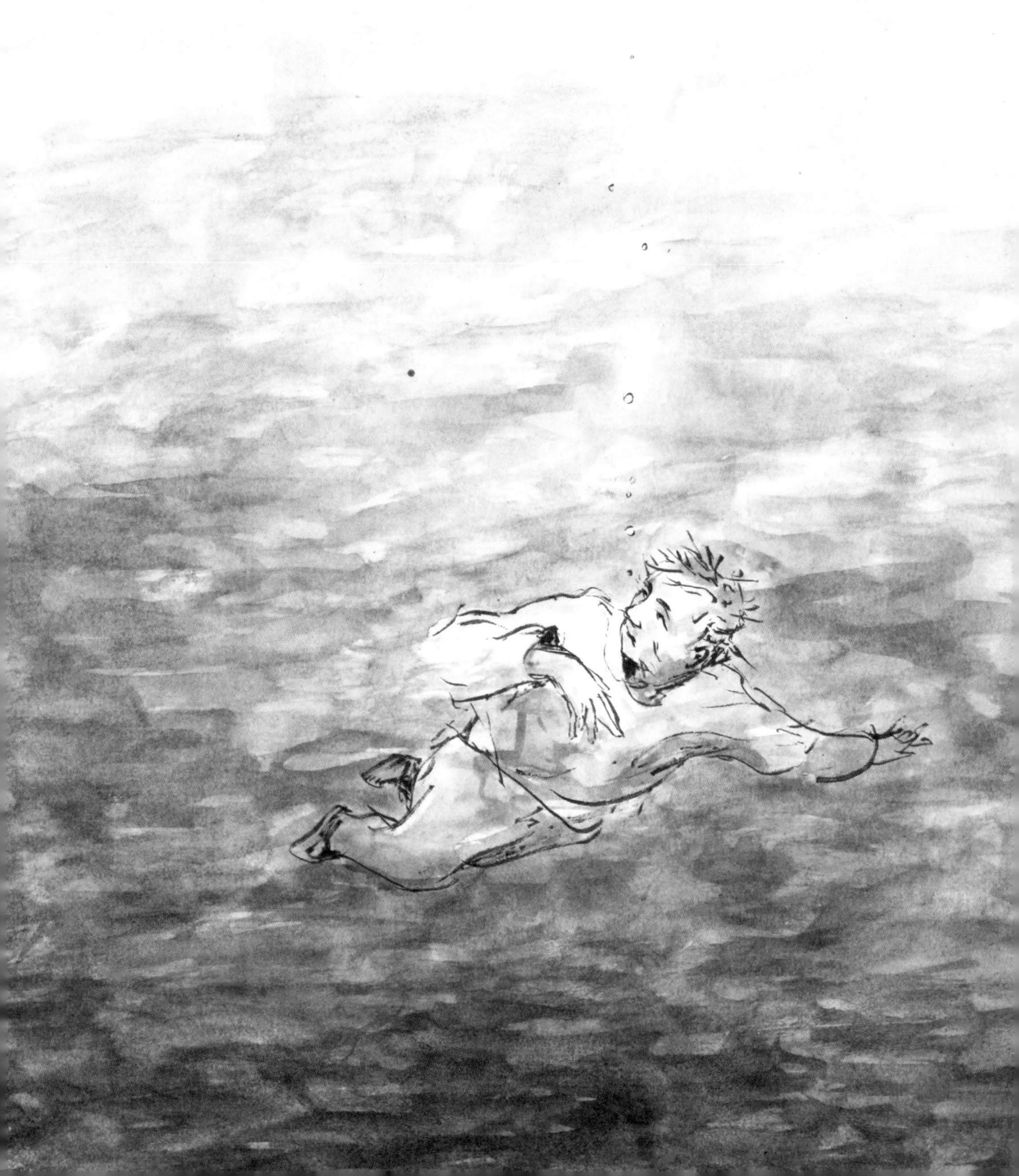

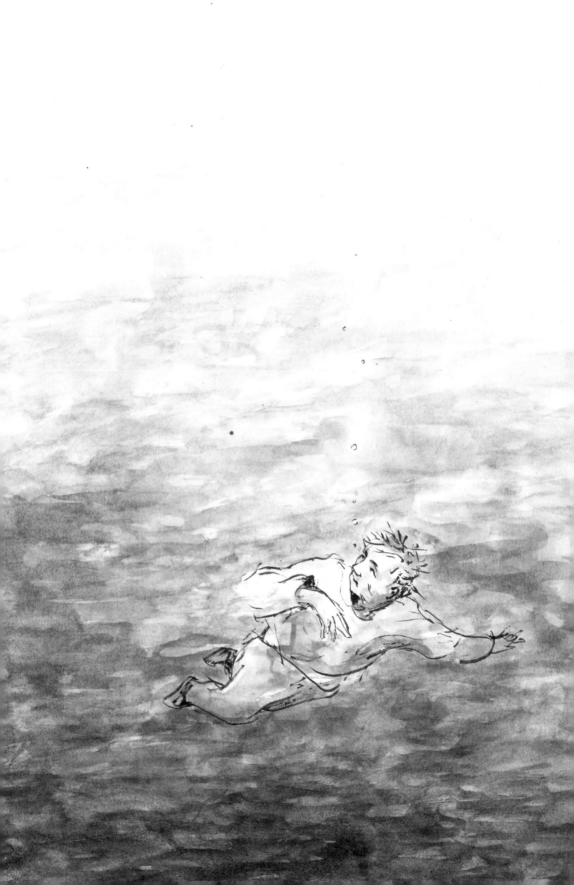

This is a story about madness. About a part of my life where there's no harmony or good judgment, only random forms of madness among the thousands of possibilities of madness. I just want the story to be honest. I can promise you, it's uncomfortable.

My memory swings between the sharp and the blurry. I'm not sure if the events happened the way I'm telling them, or not. Maybe this story is true only in my own world of noises. In any case, that's what matters, right?

Mine isn't the kind of story where, after a long, hard climb, I'll finally reach the summit with a defiant smile on my face. This is not a story about personal victory. It's simply part of an attempt to build collective meaning out of all these traces of madness.

Until now, I've been able to maintain a certain chronological order. Not anymore. It wouldn't even make much sense to do so. This is not a tragedy-to-redemption narrative. Nobody is going to save me in the end.

This hit me, first, as an intuition, and later as a certainty. It was solid ground on which to set foot.

I remember pretty clearly what the psychiatrist in the mental health clinic said. . . .

YOU HAVE A DISEASE, AND YOU NEED TO UNDERSTAND THAT IT'S SERIOUS AND IT'S CHRONIC. NOW, TRY TO REMAIN CALM TO PROCESS ALL OF THIS.

WHAT YOU'RE EXPERIENCING IS GOING TO AFFECT EVERY ASPECT OF YOUR LIFE—SCHOOL, WORK, RELATIONSHIPS. YOU CAN'T AVOID IT. WE'RE HERE TO HELP YOU.

YOU NEED TO ACCEPT THAT, FOR THE TIME BEING, YOU'LL HAVE TO LIVE WITH YOUR PARENTS. IT'S THE BEST THING FOR YOU RIGHT NOW. THERE'S GOOD MEDICATION, YOU'LL SEE. WHAT WE NEED TO FOCUS ON IS THAT YOU HAVE THE BEST POSSIBLE QUALITY OF LIFE.

And here's the thing: she said nothing about getting well, stopping the suffering, finding a cure, understanding what was going on, or learning how to handle this new reality that was crashing in on me. . . . Instead of advising me on how to get out of this fresh hell, she spoke about having "a certain quality of life." And to reach that miserable objective, there was medication.

WE'LL BE TRYING DIFFERENT ONES, TRUST ME. . . .

There were different diagnoses and medications earlier. But then, I was very careful not to mention the voices.

I left the consultation with a big secret, an ugly sentence, and a bunch of prescriptions in my pocket for psychotropic medications. But something here didn't quite add up. I was experiencing the kind of confusion that was caused by something more than the bad news I'd just been given. The interview with that middle-aged woman with the tired expression had ended abruptly. A heavy metallic door had closed behind me. Clack! The die was cast. You go into the consultation room immersed in fear and confusion, and you come out of it turned into a madman, with all your paperwork in order.

It seemed unbelievable to me that someone could come up with a diagnosis in less than three-quarters of an hour. It's that doubt that set me on the journey to where I am today.

At first, I sank into an ocean of curses, grief, and anguish. It was the classic "Why me?" scenario, in which nobody else had ever experienced what I was going through.

Then, little by little, feelings of doubt started to develop in the back of my mind. What tests did they have me take to confirm that I have an incurable disease? None. Not a single empirical or laboratory test was done, nothing that looked like an x-ray or a blood test. It's human to doubt things. In fact, human beings are the way we are largely because we harbor doubts. The problem, then, lies in the fact that, once your medical record shows that you've been diagnosed with a psychiatric disorder, any suspicion becomes an automatic indicator that confirms your insanity.

Reading, asking questions, seeking out people in the same situation . . . when you do all of these things, it can become something that gives you away.

No matter how messed up it is to say this, being middle class gave me some real advantages. I knew medical students, I had access to university libraries, and I had plenty of time to myself. Not everybody has these kinds of resources when they are only nineteen.

I needed to learn about the experiences of other people who were hearing voices like me.

I had a feeling (and this was borne out in time) that I would be able to find the tools I needed to trace my own path forward, one that was different than the path my psychiatrist had set me on. Here's what I did:

1. I read a lot of psychiatry books. 2. I read the books that question the psychiatry books I had just read. 3. I sought out people and public conversations that would help me change the narratives that medicine had put in front of me.

When you look at it this way, it might seem simple, but it really isn't. Today, after all these years, I'm still educating myself, reading, listening, seeking alternatives. I'm still searching for people and projects that temporarily relieve my feelings of bleakness and fatigue. I question everything—even what seems to align with how I've been thinking about madness and its relationship to society. I accept no closed paradigms, no categorical interpretations—nothing that looks like a diagnosis or a sentence. The human mind is too complex to be reduced to an instruction manual. I am dedicated to searching, to clearing a path and advancing slowly.

There is no map. Or rather, there is one; but it becomes visible only as you walk through it.

And, therefore, it will always be unfinished.

At first, the answers are slow to arrive. In time, we find the clues and tools we need to interpret what has happened. "In the beginning was the psychotic break." That was the first line of the rest of the story.

The psychotic episode is usually experienced with the false certainty that its uniqueness makes it incommunicable. Most crises, however, have a few things in common.

I am referring, here, to the kinds of experiences that cause psychological suffering. It's important to make this distinction because some people who have hallucinations don't always experience them as either traumatic or overwhelming. The content of a person's hallucinations is key.

The first thing to bear in mind is that they come as a violent disruption. Like the blow of an ax, splintering your sense of self. The second thing is that most others often perceive these experiences as an attack against what's normal. What's normal for them.

(Once I burned my feet by rubbing them against the parquet floor during one of my episodes.)

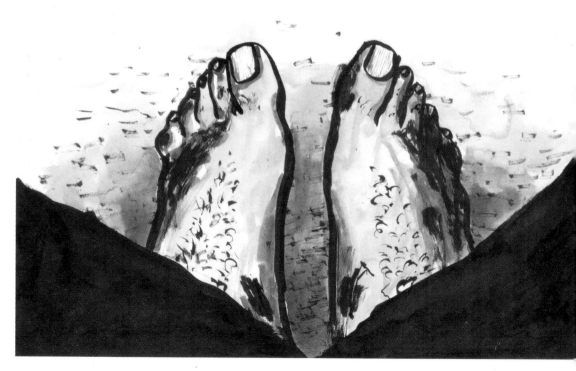

This is how the narrative is shaped for many the first time
they suffer a psychotic crisis. This is why the way people around you respond is so
important in those first moments. After. . .

. . . admission to
the hospital, . . .

. . . receiving your
diagnosis, and . . .

. . . starting medication.

It happens quite often that family members (parents, almost always) stigmatize this
experience. And there are *so* many ways of doing so. In my case, which is by no means
the most messed up one I've encountered, my family simply denied what was happening.

I have never asked them if they understood what was happening to me. (And I am
afraid that at this point I never will, unless this book serves as a convenient pretext).
But I guess they were clinging to the "It'll be over soon" way of thinking.

When you are punished for having an episode, or when they pretend it didn't happen, you tend to internalize strong feelings of guilt. This happens time and time again.

You suffer twice: The first time because of what is happening to you. The second time because of how others make you feel. Like you have failed them.

You have failed them so much that you might even be punished for it. . . .

They admit you to the hospital, they send you off to live with a relative, they seize your bank accounts, they deny your legal rights, they hide you from the rest of the family, they make you feel invisible. You are guilty and you don't know why. At a certain point, it feels like a monster is devouring your life.

You want to run, but where to?
Your muscles are stiff, your body doesn't
respond. You try to think, but it feels like
there are little pieces of crushed glass in
the folds of your brain. You shut your eyes
tight. You count and you breathe, one, two,
three, four, five, six. . . . You open your
eyes to see several boxes of psychotropic
drugs piled up on your bedside table.

Antipsychotics and various tranquilizers.
You're guilty of something. Something big.
You're guilty. It's a shame that it took me
so long to realize something so obvious: all
of those pills couldn't, can't, and never will
be able to fight this certainty.

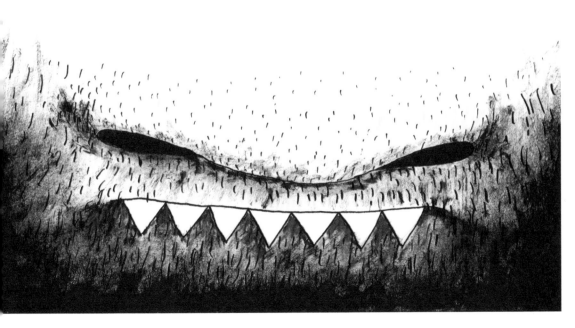

Any secrets you have that are worth keeping—I mean, *real* secrets—are but another way of looking at the world. There are no tricks or magic. Just another "way of seeing" that has been forgotten or voluntarily silenced.

My secret lies in the fact that I have no intention of ignoring my voices. To deny their existence is something I can't afford to do.

They are a part of me, and I have no interest in pretending to be someone I'm not.

This is, quite simply, mental health in its literal sense: I reject more doses of confusion than the ones the world has already foisted upon me without my consent. I am a guy who hears voices inside his head. I can hide this at work or with my family, but I can't hide it from myself.

The voices are a part of me. A part I need to control, yes, but also a part of me that has played an essential role in my daily life for more than fifteen years. The voices are a part of my identity, for better and for worse. There's no doubt about it. I hate them. I'm afraid of them.

They've managed to fuck up my life. They've overpowered me.

They give me orders.

They make promises.

They make threats.

Nevertheless, and despite what psychiatrists, psychologists, and even other people who also experience auditory hallucinations might think, my voices have been the most reliable resource I've ever had to help me face what is happening to me, to try to understand it, to try to change. They are not a disease in and of themselves; they are a trail that allows me to trace my steps to the origin, to a symptom that tells me that something is not going right.
That's it really (and it's no mean feat).
It took me many years to understand this.
Many years.

digression, n. Departure or deviation from the subject in discourse or writing; an instance of this.

—*Oxford English Dictionary*

I've made it this far with my story, despite having detoured quite a few times. To talk about madness isn't easy. Even less so, to talk about one's own madness. And to draw it, to draw the life that someone else is narrating, I'm fairly certain it must be pretty fucking difficult. However, after several meetings with Mario, after making notes, doing sketches, sending emails, and having phone conversations, the story began to take shape. Began to gel. And that has made us both, scriptwriter and illustrator, feel like this is *our* story. Which felt very good.

But this is a digression. A detour. A pause. And it's meant to say something important. We don't know what shape our story is going to take in the coming pages. But what we *do* know, what we can say with absolute certainty, is that, from this moment on, the story is going to be told and drawn in a different way.

And the reason for this has to do with some traumatic personal events for those of us caught up in this story. First, my partner developed a frightening protracted illness. It has impacted the last year and a half of my life. When she started to recover, it seemed wise to stop testing the patience of our selfless illustrator and resume the project. We had planned for Mario to come to my house for the weekend so that we could catch up. Twenty-four hours before he was due to arrive, I learned that he was in a horrendous bike accident—a car had run him over. He was admitted to the hospital with a severe traumatic brain injury. His helmet was smashed into a million pieces, and his body was thrown onto the car that had rammed him. It took him almost two months to recover, after which we were finally able to have our meeting. The little blood clots that had formed on his brain were reabsorbed by his body and by his unfathomable will to recover. Thus, we pick the thread up where we left it. But it will never be what we once thought it would. And this is good. Because change is always good.

Yesterday we had dinner, Mario, my partner, and I. Each of us has experienced events that dramatically altered our relationship with reality. This feeling of being distant from what is real has, ironically, brought the three of us closer together. The violence of an impact, the secondary effect of medication, the psychosis. For a moment, everything we felt, collectively, held together. Like leaves hanging from a branch that are rocked by the wind. Sometimes, things are much simpler than we expect them to be: you have a bad experience, and then you just want to move on and embrace life.

Mario picks up his felt-tip pens and brushes, while I start typing words on the screen.

Let's carry on.

I disagree with everyone who thinks that what goes on in my head has nothing to do with my life or the world I live in. I disagree with those who say categorically that it all has to do with a chemical imbalance and genetic heritage.

In the last fifteen years, I have sought out each and every scientific article and news alert announcing a new, infallible diagnostic test for schizophrenia, or the existence of any kind of biological marker for this so-called mental illness. And I find myself at the same place I was at the very beginning. There is nothing to see once the smoke clears. There's no tangible evidence.

Nevertheless, after all these years, after everything I've read and all the people I've met, I have reached a conclusion that helps me see things differently: nobody I know who has gone mad is being treated all that well by life.

There is a connection between the social component of psychological suffering and the people who experience it. My eyes can't make much sense of chemical structures and DNA sequences—and even if they could, that wouldn't change my daily life in the least. But my eyes can certainly learn new ways of looking at the world to help me make decisions.

I see two ways forward. On the one hand, I don't know how you can confront psychological pain without intervening in the social issues at the root of the pain. . . .

. . . confronting the structures of society, its power relations, its sorrows. . . . This great black hole that presents itself as the only possible reality. It needs to be overcome. But social change moves so slowly that it often has little effect on an individual's life.

That's why it's necessary to take a different route, and one that helps you to build up your inner resistance over time.

Through self-observation, self-defense, self-criticism: challenge and change. This is what makes you want to stay alive.

Ultimately, life is like a tightrope. And for those of us who
want to embrace life to its fullest, the only way of doing that
is to walk the tightrope. It's absurd wondering if that's a good
thing or a bad thing. It just is.

The tightrope walker will fall in any number of ways. The key to survival lies in knowing all the possible ways of getting back up. That's the only way I know to face suffering, whether it's psychological or not.

What we refer to as "mental health problems" is human suffering. Just one form among many others, even if it's unique in some ways, especially from a social perspective. After all, it's the kind of pain that exceeds medical knowledge.

Something as striking as hearing voices, which you see a lot of in literature and movies, is a completely valid human experience. An experience that you have to confront, when something breaks, and it becomes a problem for the person hearing the voices.

I'd rather think of myself as
a madman than a sick man.
Madness can be something almost
indefinable. At its core, it is pain,
an unfamiliar place we visit, but
also a place we can leave. Mental
illness is something else: a firm
belief that, even if it can't be
determined empirically, you think
you're broken beyond repair. There
is nothing you can do about it other
than to wait for the end.

As for me, I'd rather think that madness is an adaptive strategy that failed.
An attempt to keep on living by taking a wrong path that distances you from
the world. The result is this: you find yourself knocked down on the ground,
and you need to find a way to be standing again. Even if you know that you
might be knocked down a couple more times.

The first thing to do is to establish a baseline. Something objective in the middle of so many disproportionate emotions and altered perceptions. I can tell you mine: it's the conviction that people are fucked. And with the passing of time, it only gets stronger. Maybe you think this is cliché. For me, it opens the door to two ideas that I believe are essential. The first one is that society tends to drive people crazy . . .

. . . and the second one is that what happens to me, as intimate as that may be, also happens to other people.

This is not a memoir. This isn't about giving you the story of my life, blow by blow, of getting it all out there with total impunity. I'm just trying to string a few beads together so that I can make my point, even if it exposes me.

I alluded to this earlier, and now it's time to say a bit more. I want to explain something to you . . . what's more, I want to try to convince you of something: in the midst of fear and uncertainty, it is *others* who allow us to discover different ways of living. We're all afraid. We all feel uncertainty. Life is a problem. It's a collective problem we all have a share in. And this is something we all must learn over the years. Something that goes beyond madness.

Because if what we call "psychosis" fractures measurements and distances, what can help us pick up our broken pieces and pull us out of our isolation and suffering is solidarity, friendship, and love. These open up the way to life.

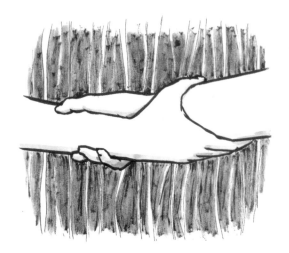

There is a kind of excess in love, in the struggle, in the affection. A force that barges in and undoes what has been done, giving us new possibilities, gesturing toward futures that are written neither in clinical reports nor on prescriptions. And if I've tried to explain what it's like to hear voices in your head, I now need to tell you about how I've tried to understand and accept them so that I can ultimately disobey them.

The ability to get back up after you've had a big fall (or after you have simply toppled to the ground like a tree cut off at its roots) is directly related to the strength and number of hands nearby to help you up.

This is true for recovering from a physical illness, for facing an eviction, for handling a conflict at work, for dealing with economic hardship, and so forth. And of course it's true for everything related to mental health.

The fact that I'm sitting here writing these lines is all thanks to others and the relationships we have. It is this human network that has allowed me to come back every time I got lost. It's as simple as that. Obviously, I'm not talking about family, or at least not the biological one. I'm talking about the network of relationships I have developed since my late teens. All of the shared and common bonds. It's about time I mentioned them—along with the things that erode them.

Even if some of these people retreated in the toughest times—and some literally told me to fuck off, even if I was the one who retreated for long periods of time, someone always knocked on my door.

I hate all of those made-up sayings about luck and friendship. It's too much of a serious issue to summarize with platitudes. Ralph Waldo Emerson wrote that the only way to have friends is by being one. If it was that easy, I'd have lost fewer friends, and I wouldn't be so proud of the ones I've got. I can remember, for instance, the first time in my life when I was taking large doses of medication. I sank into a state of exhaustion and a kind of selfish misanthropy.

I locked myself up in my parents' house, where I stopped bathing and spent all my time cursing my luck and hating humankind (a pretty common phase, by the way). Olanzapine put me in a daze and made me fatter by the week. I became hopelessly isolated: I stopped going out and, later, stopped picking up the phone. One day, my friend Daniel managed to get my parents to open the door, and he got into my room. . . .

GRRR, YOU CAN'T GO ON LIKE THIS, GRR, GRR, YOU'RE LETTING YOURSELF GO, GRRR, GRRR

WHERE? GRR, GRR, PEOPLE GRRR, GRRR. THERE'S NO AIR, GRRR, GRRR.

He talked, but I have no idea what he said.

Then he hugged me . . . and I felt profound revulsion. The closeness of his body felt like a deformed mass of warm dead meat pressing its weight upon my sternum. I desperately wanted that hug to be over.

When it was, he was crying. Daniel is not the kind of guy who cries often, and I doubt he has cried since that moment, seventeen years ago. He said goodbye and he didn't look back. Through the window, I saw him get into his car. Something shattered into pieces inside my head. I knew that what was happening to me couldn't be good and that I had to do something.

The boundary between being messed up and being irretrievably fucked up is drawn by a blurry line that moves constantly underfoot. On one side, life seems possible (even with all its complications and difficulties); on the other side, a dark ocean engulfs you, making it harder to get out with each passing day. Usually, there's no space between these two sides—no shades of grey, no way of escaping, step by step, from the disorder.

In a society defined by isolation and fragmentation, where people simultaneously try to sell you the virtue of wild individualism and the evilness of difference, being able to stay on the good side of the line depends on not being alone. And not being alone depends, to a great extent, on prioritizing the networks in your life, on believing that life is worth living when it's lived alongside others.

I've done an endless number of foolish things, and I've been very close to the abyss at least half a dozen times. But I care about others. I don't want to lose them. In some imprecise way, I've always known that my health is also about the others in my life. And that has saved my ass.

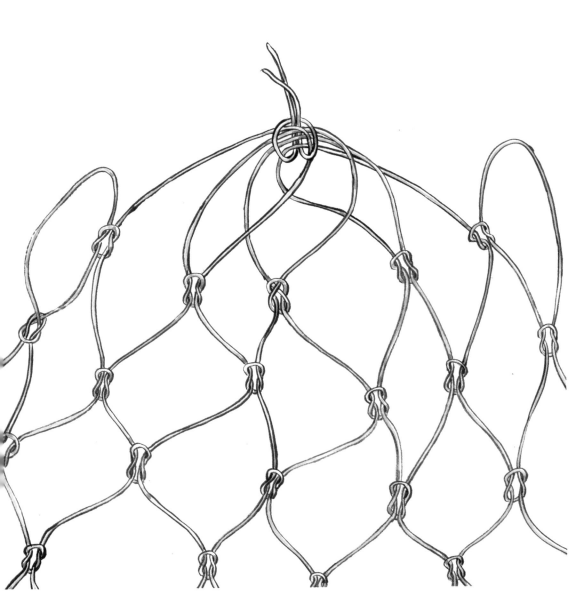

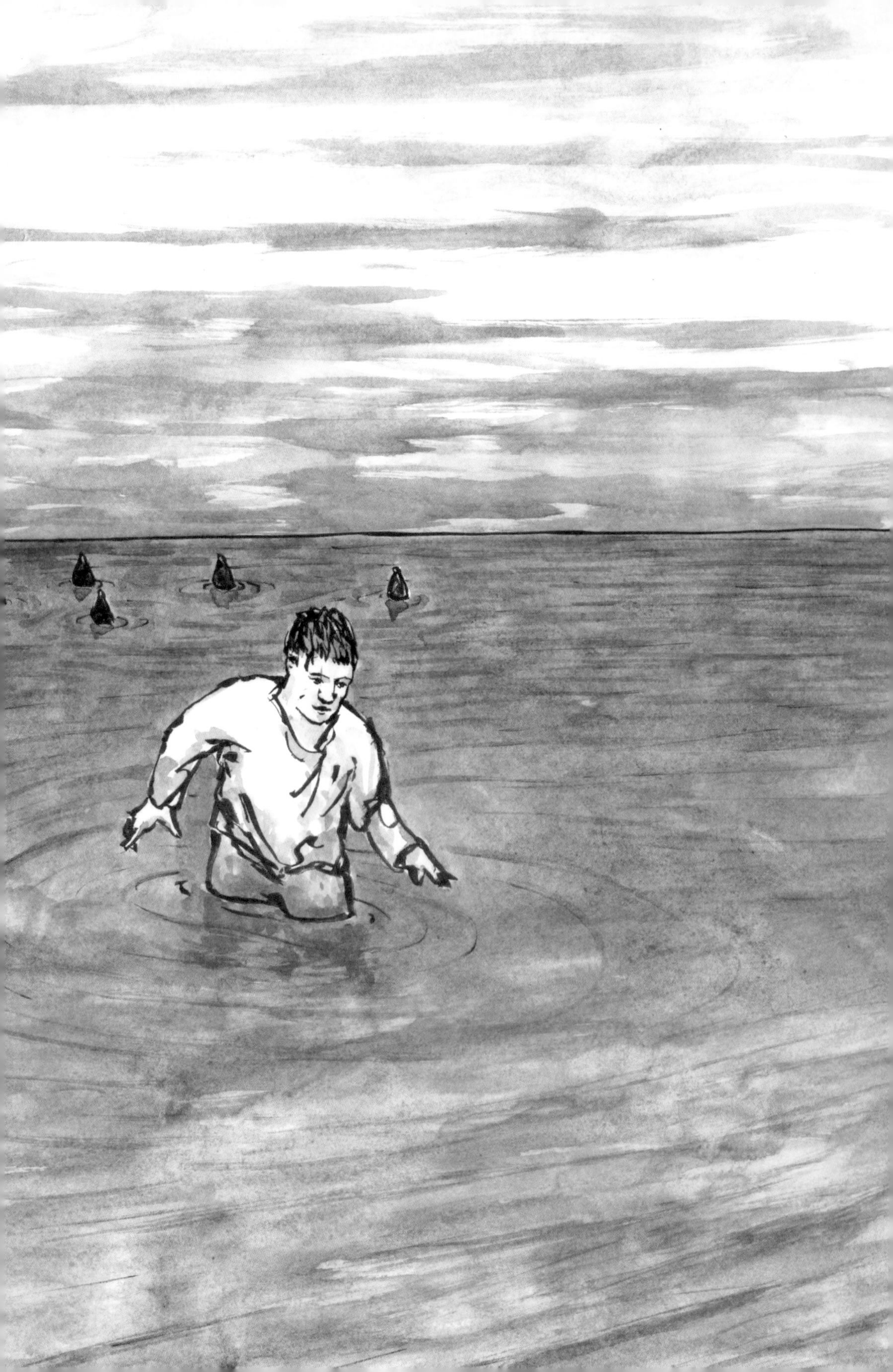

It's tempting to want to show you the full range of my wounds. To dig into them. To try, ultimately, to make you see how much this hurts . . .

However, all I'll say is that there is beauty in the stitches, which I have been able to discover because of my own appreciation for what is unusual and different.

It's the sutures that finally allow a wound to close—wounds that would otherwise remain open, leaving the body exposed and unable to heal. These stitches pierce the flesh with precision so that it does not reopen. The needle sews on both sides of the wound so that it can seal. Isn't there something beautiful about this?

To see those stitches and to show them to others prevents us from getting trapped in the loop. It's because of the stitches . . .

. . . that you move forward.

It's far too easy to be overgenerous with oneself, to make excuses. The next logical step would be to expect others to do the same. And any relationship based on this reduces life to nothing more than a sham. It's hard to get out of that toxic loop by yourself. Only Baron Münchhausen could get out of a swamp by pulling himself up by his own ponytail!

In 2009, when I was surfing the web for information about auditory hallucinations, I stumbled upon something incredible: the first worldwide Hearing Voices Congress in Maastricht, Netherlands.

I was already familiar with some of the material disseminated by the international network Intervoice. Their publications have been very helpful for me. But the idea of a conference and workshops to share and learn from each other was something entirely different.

I participated in the second conference the following year, which was held in Nottingham, England. But I didn't go alone—I wouldn't have been able to. I was dragged there by what I consider to be one of the most generous acts of love I have ever experienced. My ex-partner took me. She booked the tickets and signed us up, and she managed to get us an interpreter. She sacrificed her time, her energy, and the little money she had to take me there by the hand.

Cristina's logic for doing so was clear and simple.

THERE IS A HEARING VOICES CONFERENCE, AND WE ARE GOING. WE'LL LISTEN AND WE'LL LEARN ABOUT WHATEVER THE HELL IT IS THEY'LL SAY THERE. . . .

THERE WILL BE PEOPLE FROM ALL OVER THE WORLD WHO ARE GOING THROUGH EXACTLY WHAT YOU'RE GOING THROUGH. . . ."

When you've got nothing to lose and a whole lot to gain, any attempt to squirm out of it seems pointless. She had the determination I lacked.

We made the trip. Neither of us likes to fly. In fact, she likes it less than I do. It was strange to arrive at the legendary Sherwood Forest, Robin Hood's refuge, and find a Starbucks there, and a convention center, restaurants, stores, and some sort of air-conditioned water park under a glass dome.

All of this smack dab in the middle of a huge mass of trees and English fog. I guess all of this gave the place a certain air of unreality. It was a "trip" in every sense of the word. My memory only keeps scattered thoughts, fragments of conversations, and emotions, as if they were sparks and splinters. And even though I didn't know how to cherish it at the time, now I know that going there was one of the good things I've done in my life.

One of the most important things about that trip was shifting the conversation from the use of psychiatric language to a more intimate one, fragile and close. A living language that provides warmth, and where more people fit in.

The ideas I had read about—that voices are real for the people who hear them and are a valid experience—stopped being a mere theory and became something more tangible.

You could hear it, smell it, taste it. . . . You could almost hold it in your hands.

The world as I knew it changed overnight. No matter what was said or not said in the talks and workshops, you didn't have to conceal things or explain yourself.

Stuttering during the sessions.

Hugging a tree at the end of a presentation.

Bouncing a knee agitatedly while listening.

Or falling asleep under the influence of medication. Everything was all right, everything was perfectly broken.

I learned that space can be built for speaking the unspoken.

That victims of sexual violence often hear voices afterward.

That the life expectancy of people diagnosed with schizophrenia is reduced by twenty-five years.

That, just like some people hear negative voices, others hear voices full of encouragement and compassion.

Or that there's a whole lot of experiential knowledge available to help strategize about the day-to-day.

I remember the high-pitched voice of a Scottish activist. We had a terrible time understanding her accent, and she talked in such a rush. In one of the hallways, she asked me:

DO YOU HAVE SERVICE IN THE SUBWAY IN YOUR TOWN?

YES. CAN YOU TALK ON YOUR PHONE ON THE TRAINS . . . ?

PARDON?

ON SOME LINES. BUT . . . I DON'T UNDERSTAND. . . .

YOU HEAR VOICES. . . . PEOPLE WHO HEAR VOICES USUALLY HAVE A HARD TIME IN THE SUBWAY. IF THERE COMES A TIME WHEN YOU AREN'T FEELING WELL AND THE ANXIETY IS GETTING WORSE . . .

. . . THE BEST THING TO DO IS TO GET OFF AT THE NEXT STOP. YOU CAN TAKE YOUR PHONE OUT AND TALK TO YOUR VOICES. . . .

TELL THEM TO SHUT UP AND LEAVE YOU ALONE. CALL THEM ALL THE NAMES YOU WANT AS YOU EXIT THE SUBWAY. . . .

PEOPLE ARE USED TO HEARING OTHERS ARGUE ON THE PHONE. TRUST ME, IT WORKS.

Over the course of those few days, my own voices were more bitter than normal. They were getting louder and clearer. It's because of them that I have lapses in memory about the conference. I can't say that it was an enjoyable experience—at least that was not the overriding sense I had down in Sherwood Forest.

Feeling guilty for wasting everyone's time and money

I can't listen to this talk.
YOU'RE NEVER GOING TO SUCCEED
YOU'RE NEVER GOING TO SUCCEED
YOU'RE NOT LIKE THEM

I paid a price for being there. Now I realize how little it cost me. On the last day in a workshop about the dynamics of group sessions where people share their experiences (among equals, without facilitating professionals), I was struck by something someone said:

WHEN PEOPLE JOIN GROUPS, THEIR VOICES BECOME MORE AGGRESSIVE, MORE VIOLENT

It's something that happens when you start fighting with your voices for control of your life, when you lose that first speck of fear.

Because that's what it's all about—getting control and gaining autonomy. Feeling human. Something we all know and need.

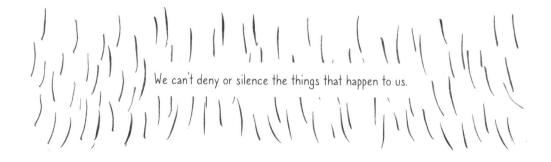

We can't deny or silence the things that happen to us.

My voices are buoys. They float on the dark sea to warn me of dangerous places.

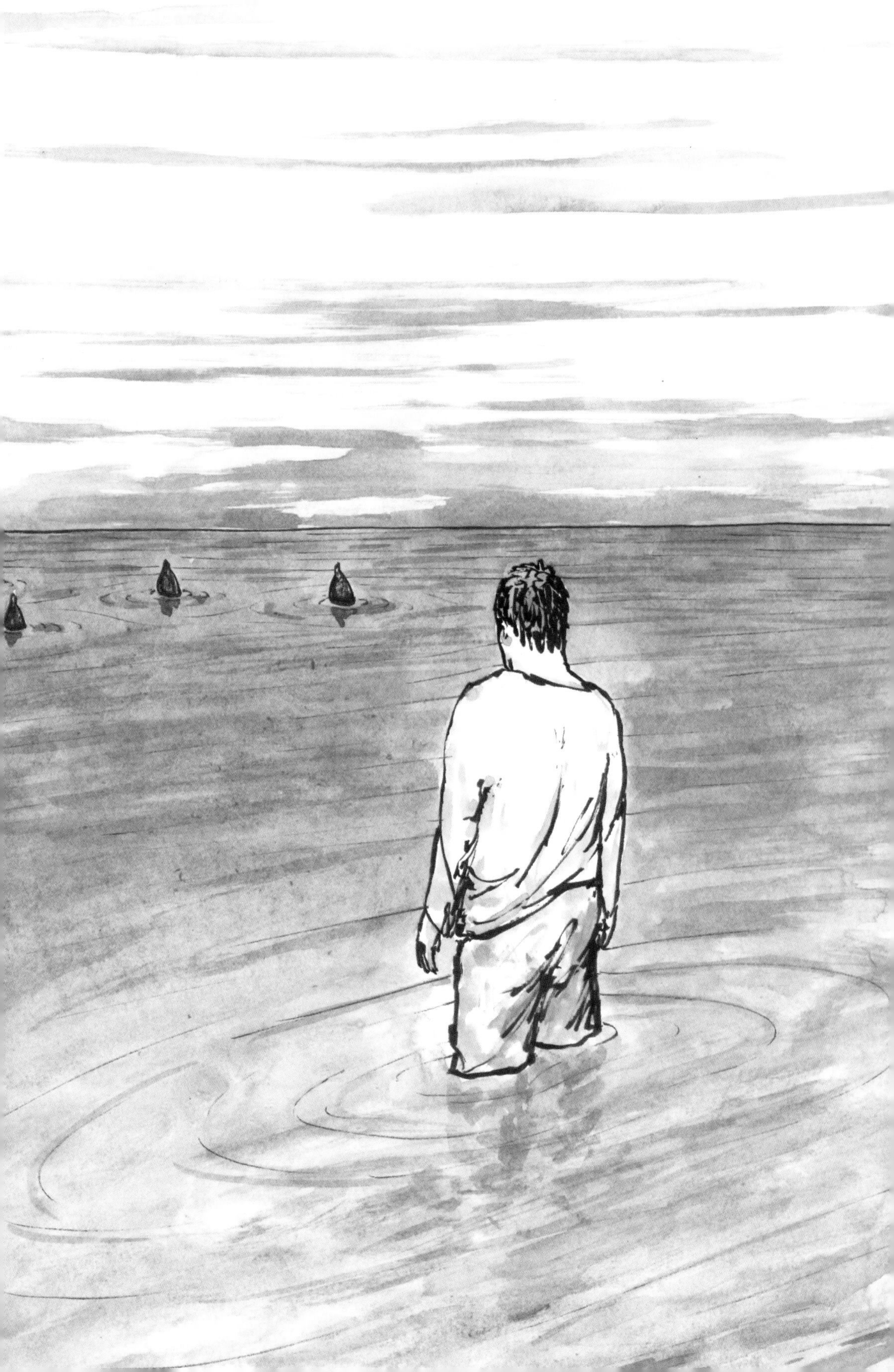

Back home, I spent several months splashing around in the warm waters of confusion. I was digesting. Later on, I came to understand how the experience had affected me: I realized that I had more respect for myself.

I heard this in Nottingham: "We have far more fear when we're alone." That might seem like an obvious statement, but it isn't in the slightest. We humans tend to be alone, regardless of whether or not we've been in a mental health clinic. It's almost a social condition of our times. That generally means that, even if we share key aspects of our lives with others, we don't truly know each other. We don't talk. And above all, we don't listen to one another.

Support groups try to change that.

To understand the meaning and function of support groups, you have to let go of some preconceived ideas. Forget group therapy. Forget the scenes that come to mind from movies or TV series. Think of support groups as more like union meetings, where you can share your problems and discomfort with those around you; or like neighborhood groups that form to protest the closing of a local outpatient clinic; or like a group of homeowners who come together when the bank is threatening to foreclose. . . .

There are many kinds of support groups. They can be open or closed. Maybe they have admission requirements; maybe they don't. They might be centered on a particular experience or a condition, like hallucinations, for example, or relationship problems. They might need a temporary facilitator, or they might be entirely autonomous. They can hold meetings in health or community centers. In spite of this variety, support groups all have one thing in common: they are safe spaces where you can talk about the unspoken or the unspeakable, and you can do it one on one, on level ground.

Therein lies the true antidote for social cannibalism.

The support group concept is simple and complicated at the same time. Simple, because humans have assembled in groups for millions of years. Complicated, because we are not used to listening, to sharing without judging, and to following mutually agreed upon terms of social engagement. It's about recovering a culture that has been taken from us. Making the world stop. Disengaging ourselves from its onslaughts, stepping off the merry-go-round, and turning off our mobile phones. To create something else.

After all, who really knows anything about madness? About delirium? About the voices that speak inside our heads? We do. The ones who survive madness. The ones who are delirious. The ones who hear things that others don't. Each one of us is an expert in our own reality.

What's more, each of us is *the only possible expert.*

Clinical knowledge is not a shared knowledge. There is a need for collective spaces in which to explore what hasn't been said. To rehearse new ways of relating, and to discuss everything we have learned from one another that has helped us to survive. To look through a crack for other worlds where it's okay to be broken . . . and where it's not seen as a social defeat.

EAT WELL AND GET THE BEST POSSIBLE SLEEP.

THE DIAGNOSES HAVE NOTHING TO DO WITH WHO YOU ARE AS A PERSON.

I WOULD CUT MYSELF BECAUSE IT SOOTHED ME. I DIDN'T WANT TO DIE, I JUST WANTED TO BE CALM.

GODDAMN RAT RACE. WORK, THE HOUSE, NEVER ENOUGH MONEY. LIKE A HAMSTER ON A WHEEL. DOES IT MAKE YOU LOSE YOUR MIND?

THEY'RE THE MAD ONES. THEY'RE THE MAD ONES. BLOODY HELL. MAD ONES.

GOD LOVES US. MADNESS IS SIN.

THE MEDIA LIES. PEOPLE WITH PSYCHIATRIC DIAGNOSES ARE LESS VIOLENT THAN NORMAL PEOPLE.

WHEN I START ASKING FOR FORGIVENESS, START SAYING "I'M SORRY" MORE AND MORE, THAT'S WHEN THE PATH AHEAD GETS TWISTY.

I DRAW. I DRAW EVERY DAY AND I HAVE NO FUCKING IDEA WHY. IT JUST FEELS GOOD.

I COULDN'T HANDLE MY VOICES. SO I STARTED NOTICING THE FEELINGS THAT WERE ATTACHED TO THEM, AND THEN I COULD DEAL WITH THEM.

IT'S REASSURING WHEN YOU REALIZE THAT NO ONE CAN REALLY KNOW EXACTLY WHAT SOMEONE ELSE IS THINKING.

PSYCHOSIS WILL PASS. NOBODY TELLS YOU THAT. NOBODY TALKS ABOUT PATIENCE.

OTHER PEOPLE SUFFER TOO. WHEN I'M FUCKED UP, I FORGET THAT.

TO BE REPRESSED IS TO BE SUPPRESSED.

THINK AND SMOKE JOINTS. SMOKE JOINTS AND THINK. I END UP HEARING OTHER PEOPLE'S THOUGHTS IN MY HEAD.

THEY PUT ME IN RESTRAINTS. I COULDN'T MOVE MY TORSO. I WOULD PISS AND SHIT MYSELF. THEY CALLED ME FILTHY. I CRIED. AND SOMETHING ELSE BROKE INSIDE MY CHEST.

WHEN I LOST MY JOB, THE VOICES TOOK OVER.

YOU CAN'T BE A WHORE, A DAUGHTER, AND A MOTHER. AT LEAST I COULDN'T. BETTER THAT WAY.

JESUS LOVED US, HE DIED FOR OUR SINS. AND I COULDN'T EVEN GET OUT OF BED WHEN THE ALARM WENT OFF.

I LEFT MY PARENTS' HOUSE. I WAS FINALLY ABLE TO BREATHE AGAIN. THOUGH I BECAME A LOT POORER.

TO RECOVER DOESN'T MEAN NEVER BEING FUCKED UP AGAIN. IT MEANS NEVER BEING FUCKED UP IN THE SAME WAY.

THE VOICES SEND A MESSAGE. THEY HAVE MEANING. THEY APPEARED WHEN I WAS YOUNG AND ON MY OWN, WITHOUT ANY SELF-ESTEEM. THEY RETURN WHEN THINGS ARE GOING DOWNHILL, WHEN I CARE TOO MUCH ABOUT WHAT OTHERS THINK.

BEING HOSPITALIZED WAS TOUGH, I ALMOST DIDN'T MAKE IT.

I HAVE FIVE EVIL VOICES AND ONE GOOD ONE. THE LAST ONE KEEPS ME OUT OF TROUBLE AT WORK.

IT MAKES NO SENSE TO BE DEFENSIVE WHEN NOBODY SEEMS TO CARE.

One of the issues that comes up time and time again in particularly safe settings is medication. Whether you're in group or one-on-one with someone you feel comfortable with, pills are always by your side, whether you take them or not.

And all those years taking them make you an expert in psychopharmacology.

I could write a short treatise on my adventures with psychiatric drugs. It's a complicated story and of course too long to include here. Nevertheless, as we've seen, the substances I was prescribed have had a significant impact on me.

In the beginning, I assumed medicines were a given. Later, as I started to doubt the reliability of my diagnosis, I became a lot more cautious. In the exam rooms, they talked to me about scientific facts, but as the months and years went by, I came to realize that it was all smoke and mirrors.

My voices and noises were never entirely suppressed by pills. It was especially reassuring to hear this from other people as well. We tend not to mention this so that we don't end up on even higher doses and drooling.

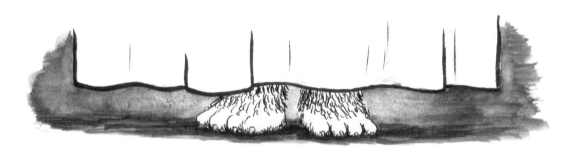

That doesn't mean that medications aren't useful. It only means they don't offer a cure. Psychiatrists can't come up with a diagnosis based on objective tests, and their drugs can't make us healthy, either.

As long as there isn't a psychiatric disorder that is undeniably linked to a biochemical imbalance, I choose to think (as do many other people who are diagnosed, or psychiatrists, psychologists, neurologists, and researchers) that these substances can produce an intoxication whose effects might prove beneficial.

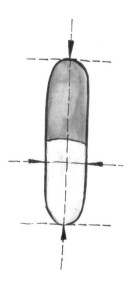

Pills (and injections, drops, inhalers, and so on) create an abnormal state of mind. They affect the nervous system and they alter the way you think, feel, and behave.

Medication stuns you: it lowers your capacity for physical, mental, and emotional activity. It's true that hallucinations and deliriums can be weakened by these drugs, making it easier to get some rest. The side effects of agitation eventually become sluggishness, something that doctors and relatives tend to appreciate.

We go back to wanting to be on firm ground. . . .

Medication "slows" the mind, and it might (though this doesn't always happen) make hallucinations and the rest feel less unsettling to the user. This can reduce suffering, but it comes at a price. . . .

On the one hand, there are the side effects, which vary from person to person and by the medication and the dosage. This is something to be concerned about, especially in the long term. Also, medication impacts the ability to think, feel, and analyze what's happening in order to overcome it.

Overcome. Recover. Get better. Remake oneself. Everyone should have access to the kind of information that will help them determine the path they want to take.

There are those who medicate.

And those who don't.

Some people medicate only in the most difficult moments.

Others keep to a regular dose.

Some needed it only once and never took it again.

Whatever the case, there is no magic formula, no instruction manual. Medication can't restore you to the way you were before (otherwise people wouldn't give up on pharmacological treatments as often as they do). There is no single way to battle madness.

From my own experience, I can say that the drugs have helped me occasionally, especially when I wasn't equipped to handle my overwhelming experiences. I can say, too, that the drugs have harmed me when I used them in high doses for an extended period of time. Not only because of how they affected me physically, when it came to sex and the ability to concentrate, but also because of how they affected me mentally, impairing memories or coloring them negatively.

I would feel even more alienated from myself. I couldn't make sense of what was happening to me, so I would lie down on the unmade bed and wait it out, hunkered down under swollen eyelids.

But the voices didn't leave me, and the will to live didn't return by itself.

I had to pave a new way for it.

Medication did not save me. It is not saving me. It won't save me. Pills are just molecules, and what is at stake here is something else: I need to learn how to move forward.

To learn, you have to accept, and it is not always easy to accept either how screwed up you are or that the universe does not revolve around your own pain.

It seems logical that if the pain is individual, the solutions will be as well. That is how the world we've grown up in works. A myopic world where collective problems are treated as personal problems. But the solutions are always the same: take this pill, go see a therapist, buy a self-help book. A market is created.

Money changes hands. The world keeps turning.

I wasn't very keen on the idea of seeing a private therapist after being treated in the public mental health system. Apart from psychiatrists, I saw a psychologist one time who offered forty-five minutes of paternalistic blather . . .

It's not easy for a 21-year-old college student with occasional jobs to afford private therapy. My girlfriend at the time was a psych major, and she connected me with a cognitive behavioral therapy master's course where they admitted patients for free. I don't remember the number of sessions, but they were few and disastrous. Summer came, and they never called me again.

This felt too much like a trial, which only increased my mistrust of clinicians. Some years later I was encouraged by a friend who knew someone who knew of an old psychoanalyst with reasonable rates in a working-class neighborhood. My memories are jumbled, but I had a distinct (and quite possibly misplaced) feeling that we hated each other from the start. I ran out of that dumpy apartment filled with dusty piles of books and never went back.

It was a long time before I could even think about sitting down with a shrink who was not the government assistance drug dealer.

But the third time is the charm, as they say. Again, it was someone else who encouraged me in this direction. After a couple of failed attempts, including someone who refused to deal with cases involving voices (which, perversely, gave me an excuse for doing nothing and wallowing further in my misfortune), a friend who had also experienced several psychotic episodes gave me the number of her former therapist. I put it off as long as I could, until I was out of excuses.

It wasn't easy at first. . . . However, for once they asked me about my *feelings* and my *life,* before getting to my symptoms, and that was reassuring.

Meaning that the hallucinations didn't seem to have a special role in and of themselves; they only mattered in relation to me. An idea that was both trivial and surprising. We started working together. And it was hard. And unconventional. . . .

To think that I could have found this kind of treatment much earlier—all the time it would have saved me. But it's pointless to worry about that. It does make sense, though, to think about the quality of the treatment we receive from public services, and what we can find in the private sector. There's a real divide between those who can afford other kinds of care and those who can't. I was only able to start private therapy after I was 30 years old and finally in a stable job.

Yet working with a therapist can be risky. Their knowledge will always be limited, and they won't be able to save you, either. One of the greatest dangers we face in therapy is that we can become dependent. I, like so many others, fell into this trap.

Over time, it started to feel strange being in that chair.

At first it was just a moment here and there. Then the feeling of strangeness finally crowded out the trust. This wasn't my place anymore. And although it hurt, I had to leave.

I suppose this happens. Getting lost and falling is part of the race. You learn from everything. Therapy is a singular space, where time stops. You undress voluntarily. You are taken care of.

The therapist listens to you, and you listen to them. You go forward. You go back. You go forward again.

It makes sense to pay a professional who can help you dissect your fear and guilt. Someone who knows what you're going through and will be by your side as your trembling hand wields the scalpel. But to combat loneliness you must go even further.

A reader pages through a book in their own time, reading along at their own pace, while for the author—the one who has lived the story and is now telling it—the passage of time feels unsettling. The past can be rough terrain to navigate. It sticks to your skin.

I'm writing this not to chronologize my daily battles, not to offer guidance to others. I'm writing this to learn something new about myself.

I guess that's the main reason why I find it so hard sitting here and staring at the screen. But you write at your own peril. There are things that move. Sometimes they just slip a fraction of an inch, and other times they jump right up and dance.

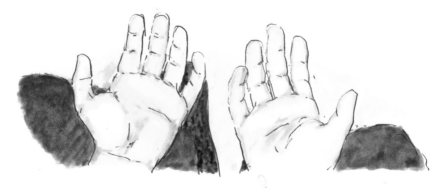

To reflect on what you know is to learn something new.
To discover patterns that connect all the fragments. . . .

Nietzsche once said that we're like flying fish. We only skim the surface of things.

Talking to other people, hearing their life stories and all the wisdom life has taught them, is the best way I know to see what lies beneath. Of course, it's not always a pleasant task.

To begin with, you must learn to listen— not only to the comforting messages that legitimize your pain and offer shelter in the storm—but you must also listen to all the hard parts, the questions that shatter the defenses you have carefully constructed in an effort to resist change.

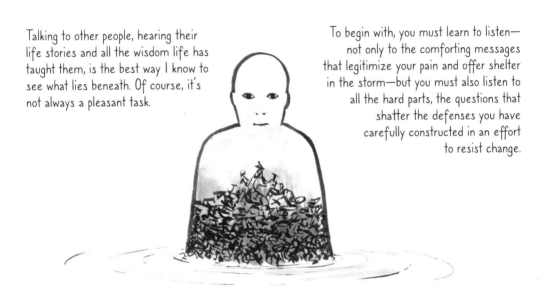

Then you need to be willing to look where nobody else wants to. To scratch at the surface. To claw your way to the inevitable realization that there's a dark side about everything in our lives—our family, gender, work, education, relationships. . . .

Finally, you have to put all of this into words. To heal yourself, so that the pain doesn't manifest in other ways.

By naming my experiences—what I do and what I feel—I can change the way I relate to my voices. I confront everything I carry within me, everything the men and women in white coats will never know how to talk about. I no longer feel the need to hurt myself in order to talk about pain. I no longer have to compare myself to others in order to figure out who I am.

If I dared to count my blessings, I would say that this long fight has been nothing but a string of acts of defiance, a slow and meticulous training in the art of saying "no."

In all the confusion, every time I choose to say no (which by definition is something intimate), it goes beyond me and affects everything around me. Every time I manage to disobey one of my voices, I grow a little stronger. Only a little, but it's enough. I have lost a good deal of my impatience with the voices. Resistance takes time but is fruitful. Resignation, on the contrary, offers the immediacy of what is already dead.

Challenging your voluntary servitude and killing your inner critic is a profound and exquisite act. It means regaining the control that has been taken from you. And it puts you in a position to be able to anticipate the outbursts of the most aggressive voices.

What once seemed impossible is no longer so . . .

. . . and the horizon becomes clear.

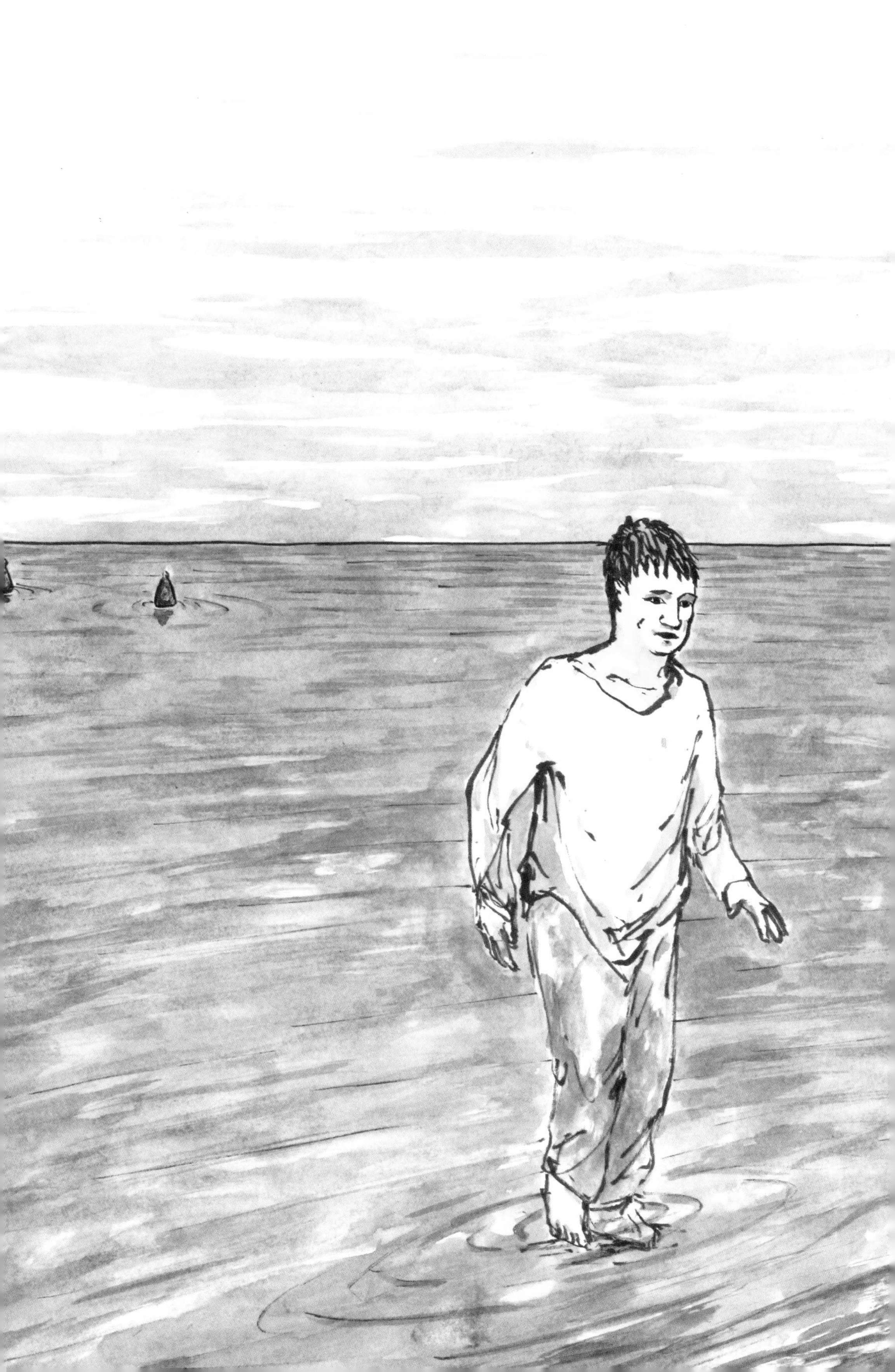

Some acts of defiance shine more than others, making life in these moments feel as liberated and as liberating as it is supposed to be. . . .

Sergio had a bad fall at work. He fell off the roof. All because the bosses skimped on safety measures.

The 400-kilometer drive to the hospital felt like 400 punches to my gut.

There were sleepless nights while we awaited the prognosis. And the delusions showed up. The noises. The voices.

"This is not the time! You have no right to be here! Get out!"
I cursed those voices and shut them the fuck up.

Why should I spend all my time and energy feeling useless and listening to these horrible insults? Why should I let them get the best of me? I hung on with all my might. And when Sergio could swallow his first bite of solid food, I knew that I was exactly where I wanted and needed to be.

The long and the short of it? Rise up and push back on yourself until you recover the ability to decide.

Slow down your thinking when your brain tries to convince you that you're a disappointment to others . . .

. . . or tries to imagine the worst. I don't always succeed, but it's a work in progress. In time . . .

How I handle the voices, the way I think about them, can alter what the voices, themselves, say. It's a one-person face-off using the language of reason.

I'm still learning to distinguish what's dangerous from what isn't, where the line is between the internal and the external. I'm still trying to manage mistrust and discouragement. Like so many others in this world, I am trying to understand myself.

Unlike so many psychiatrists, psychologists, and even some relatives of people with this diagnosis . . . I don't think there's only one way to do things. I have no interest in lecturing anyone.

And even though many of us may have similar symptoms and suffer in the same ways, each of us is unique. If I'm trying to convince anyone about anything in these pages, it's simply not to give up.

I can't tell you how many times I came this close to losing everything, and I didn't. I'm lucky.

I'll always feel dizzy.

My life has lost some of its value, and every day I work to reverse that. If I speak and write about madness, it's to question the integrity of a society that turns a blind eye to the alarming rise in mental health problems we see all around us.

In a world defined by competitiveness and simulacra, the whole notion of breaking apart seems like a logical, if not inevitable, outcome to me. Therefore, I think there is something coherent in going mad. Heresy.

However, being a casualty of the social selection process can't become an excuse for giving yourself a pass. If you're truly a victim, your legitimacy as such makes victimhood irrelevant. I try to think of myself as a survivor. If I refuse to accept the dominant narratives about madness, I have no choice but to construct new ones.

Stories in which difference doesn't marginalize us (with all the violence that goes along with that) . . .

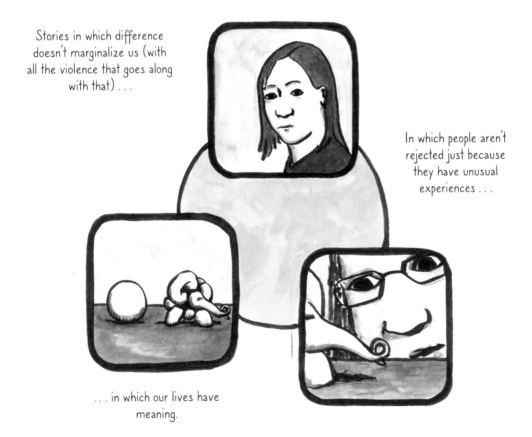

In which people aren't rejected just because they have unusual experiences . . .

. . . in which our lives have meaning.

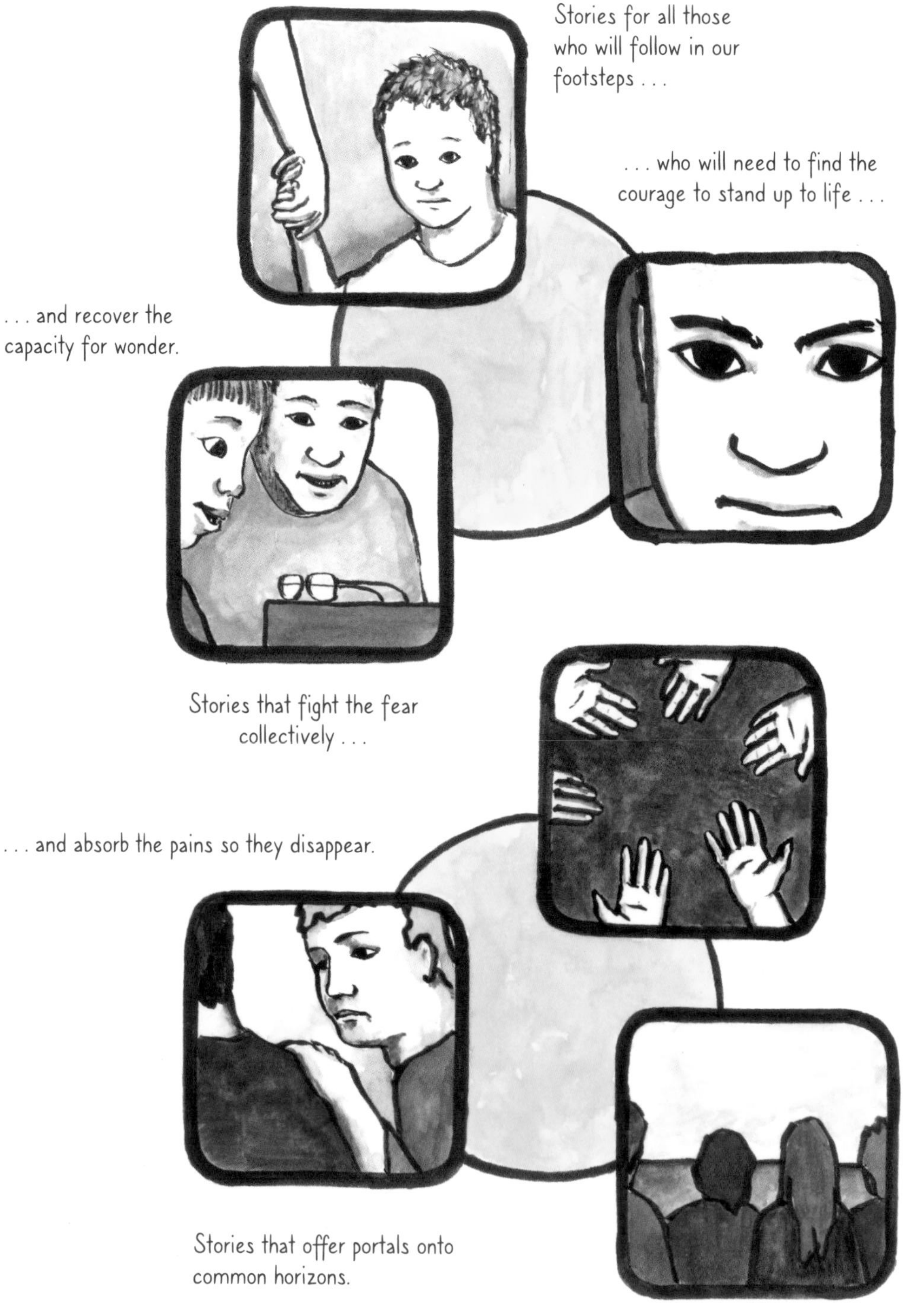
Stories for all those who will follow in our footsteps . . .
. . . who will need to find the courage to stand up to life . . .
. . . and recover the capacity for wonder.
Stories that fight the fear collectively . . .
. . . and absorb the pains so they disappear.
Stories that offer portals onto common horizons.

Stories that are ours. Like the one I'm finishing here.

I process, assimilate, digest.

I grapple with shyness.

I visit people who don't exist—
who left or died.

I smell the hospital corridors.

I hear the murmur of time
passing.

It's time to stop writing.

The eerie glow of my computer screen
has invaded my dreams. My gut hurts.

I look back to see where I've been: retracing the madness . . .

. . . of a very long journey.

This is a trip I do not have to take alone.

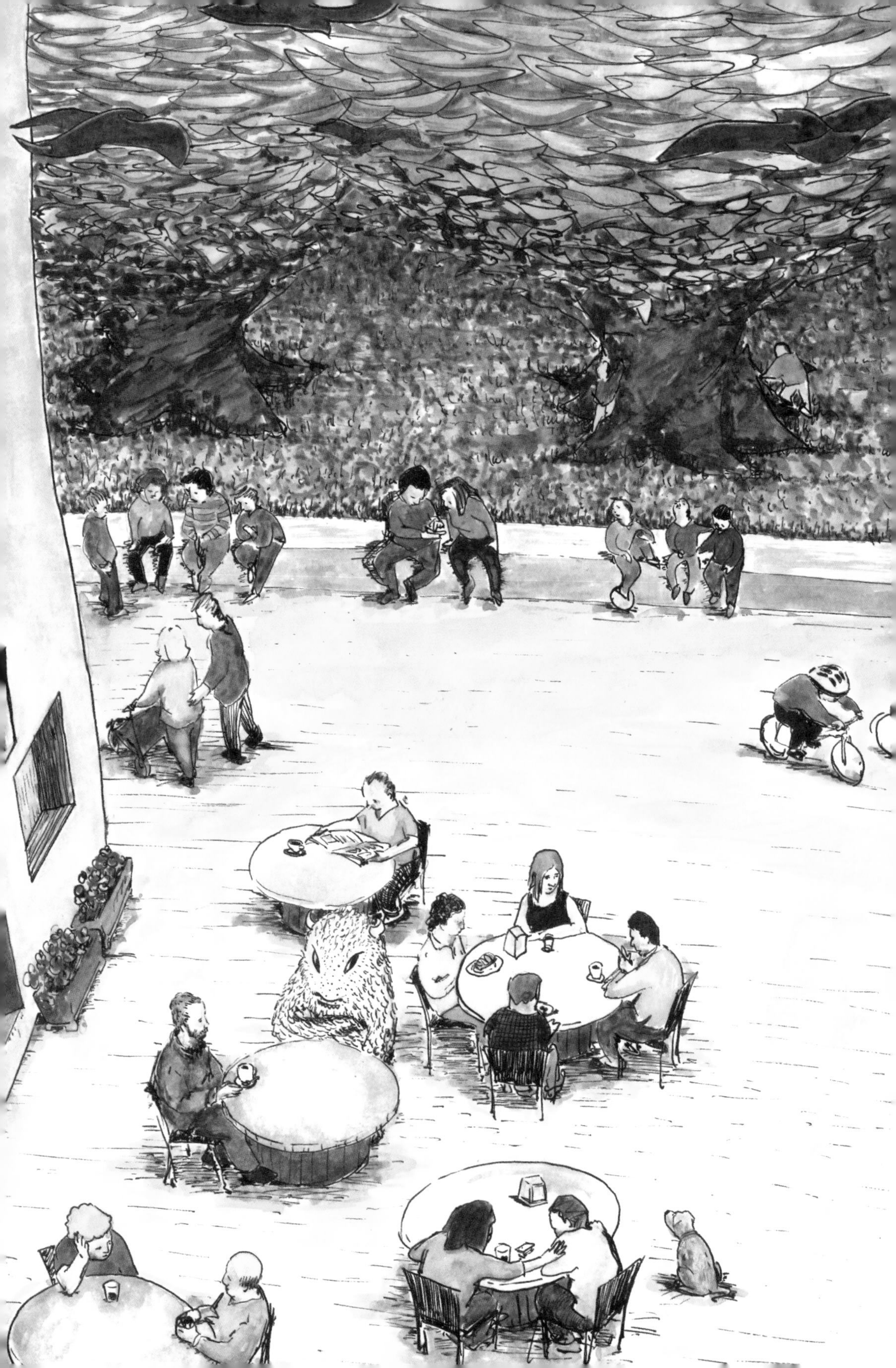

APPENDIX

In my loneliness
I have seen very clear things
that are not true.

— *Antonio Machado*

Experience comes in time. I wish I had had a book like this—a sort of navigational chart—when I first started hearing voices. I have been forced to map my own way forward, revealing a lot about my private life in the process. This makes me uncomfortable. But by now I have learned that ignorance and taboo are dangerous companions.

It's absurd to think someone else can chart the way forward for you. The tools that worked for them won't necessarily work for you. My point is that it's possible to come up with a map that helps you move ahead.

Over the years, I have learned to recognize the signs leading up to a psychotic episode with auditory hallucinations. I have collected and classified these signs. There's no fixed rule for them: sometimes they coincide, and sometimes one or another will clearly predominate. Other times they may contradict each other. I also have taken notes regarding the frequency of these episodes and their intensity, as well as memories of where I've been and how I felt. It doesn't make sense to share this subjective data here. Instead, I'll stick to more general thoughts; I'll describe how this feels through analogy. I want this to be useful.

Sensory Perceptions

Everyday sounds become roars.
Sharp or unexpected noises are particularly
shocking.

I hear the telephone ringing even though
it's not. Sometimes the ringtone is from a
specific device from the past. When I notice
it, it stops.

At sunset, I perceive colors and light in a
special way: blues gain in intensity and can
even morph into an irritating cyan.

Edges are blurred, as if I'm wearing foggy
glasses.

I see flashes and shadows in my field of vision. These aren't visual hallucinations, per se. Rather, they are ordinary phenomena, like a reflection on a screen, a piece of fuzz suspended in the air, or the passing shadow made by an object in motion, that become something extraordinary.

A familiar object seems novel, like something I've never seen before.

Familiar flavors become strange and unpleasant. Sometimes I have a puzzling, indefinable taste in my mouth that lingers for hours.

I have an acute sense of smell, and sometimes mysterious smells will appear in certain contexts. For example, I can smell my mother's potato omelet when I'm at work, or gasoline in my living room. I smell unpleasant odors on myself (sweat, feet, shit) especially when I'm in public spaces (in a work meeting, for example).

My skin becomes very sensitive. My body hair bristles easily.

Physical Symptoms

I have a weak appetite, and I'm extremely thirsty.

My muscles become tense and contract, especially in my back. I clench my hands and jaw involuntarily.

I'm sleepy all the time.

I experience extremes in sexual desire, going from indifference to overexcitement.

My respiration becomes accelerated and shallow.

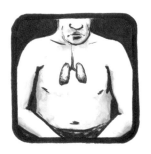

I have liquid stools and frequent bowel movements.

I lose all physical coordination and become clumsy.

I have problems with proprioception. My legs and arms hit the furniture or other people.

Psychological Symptoms

I have rituals, such as getting up at night to see if I have switched off the gas, even when I'm certain I have. And getting up later a second and third time. I check certain things a certain number of times, always in multiples of three. It feels like I've forgotten something important.

I become superstitious.

I get confused, and I can't concentrate. That's why I get lost watching movies or TV series. I miss nuances in the dialogue. I have a hard time reading complex texts.

I become more sensitive to other people's pain or violent experiences, even in fiction.

I obsess about ruin, destruction, and misfortune. I always imagine the worst-case scenario.

Extended monologues run through my mind, extremely fast circular ramblings that have no point. I'm obsessed by certain thoughts that I can't suppress.

I can only understand things by way of comparison; my capacity for analysis vanishes.

I become hyper-creative, having multiple thoughts at the same time. I enjoy word games, and I'm witty with language.

I confuse words when speaking and writing. I swap letters around.

I expect a lot of myself.

Personal Relationships

I have trouble (more than usual) reading between the lines.

I don't get humor, especially if it's ironic humor.

I feel something like claustrophobia when I'm in large crowds.

I feel sensitive and self-centered.
I can hear what others are thinking about
me.

There's a considerable disconnect between
what I'm thinking and what I am able
to express. Quite often I'm told "I'm not
following you" or "Sorry, I've lost the thread,"
etc.

I become talkative, even verbose.

How I Manage

I rest and sleep as much as possible.

I stick to routines, especially for eating and sleeping.

I limit my screen exposure time for the phone and computer. I stopped watching television years ago.

I avoid public transport and crowds.

I carefully assess when and how to spend time with my parents.

To improve my digestion, I'm careful with what I eat.

I walk a lot and seek out open spaces.

If I feel an episode coming on, I'll let the people close to me know by texting them an (often silly) watchword.

I have pacts with certain people who agree to warn me if they note any signaling behaviors that they think I might not be aware of (such as the inability to detect irony).

I place notes at home and in the workplace, especially, to be mindful of certain harmful behaviors. I try to make these notes incomprehensible to others, by writing them in other languages (in Basque, for example, a language I don't speak). This reminds me that if I'm talking too much at work or obsessing about what other people think ... *hobeto isilik egon* (it's better to keep quiet).

The author would like to thank
Graphic Mundi for facilitating the
translation of this book into English.
Thanks also to Irene R. Newey for
her invaluable help in revising the
English translation to ensure a
rendering as faithful as possible to
the original Spanish edition.